UNIVERSITY
NIT
10 0383992 9
D1102742

WHAT DID YOU IN THE WAR, MUM?

WOMEN RECALL THEIR WARTIME WORK

Edited by Pam Schweitzer, Lorraine Hilton and Jane Moss.

Researched by Lorraine Hilton and Jane Moss. Photography by Alex Schweitzer.

Age Exchange wish to thank all the women who gave us their time and allowed us to record their stories and borrow their photographs for this project.

CONTRIBUTORS

Hilda & Ben Bennett	Mrs. Hill	Alice Stewart	T. Gorringe
Rose Mullett	Mrs. Langford	Mrs. Wright	Marie Maberley
Joy Brown	Mrs. Bessie Miller	Paula Williams	Sylvia Jacobs
Mrs. Rose Martin	Ruth Granville	Lucy Apton	Mrs. Dubus
Mrs. Valerie Moss	Mr. and Mrs. Jones	Emmy Hewlette	Mrs. Grossman
Mrs. Irene Nash	Mrs. Chaplain	Evelyn Ritchie	Eliza Eldridge
Mrs. Patricia Thom	Jean Batcham	Lisa Haddon	Lily Jane Short
Helen Parker	Mrs. Stanley	Mrs. Ivy Jones	Florrie Clayton
Ellen Harbard	Maria Tardios	Helen Davis	Nora Carton
Mrs. Bancroft	Mabel Kibble	Mrs. Dolores Reyes	Sam Aldous
Mrs. Dorothy Duncan	Mrs. Chuter	Vivian Prince	Mrs. Hillbeam
Daisy ''Prim'' Hawkes	Patricia Graves	Margaret Kippin	Mrs. Smith
Mrs. Crane	Mrs. Gange	Arthur Wellard	Mrs. Pitt
Mrs. Burtenshaw	Bridget McDevitt	Joan & Bill Welch	Mrs. Dixon
Mrs. Eaton	Victoria Hill	Mrs. Nightingale	Mrs. Dudley

"What Did You Do In The War, Mum?" is published by Age Exchange Theatre Company to coincide with their theatre production of the same name. The show, scripted by Joyce Holliday and directed by Pam Schweitzer, is based on the stories in this book. The book is being reissued to mark the European Year of Older People.

First published 1985.

This Edition, 1993.

Copyright © Age Exchange Theatre trust, 1985.

INTRODUCTION

What Did You Do In The War, Mum? is the result of a series of interviews with women pensioners in the London area. It charts the war-time experience of women working on munitions, in the forces, the Land Army, administration, and the service industries. Our research has involved discussions with groups of pensioners, in which slides, photographs and music have been used to stimulate reminiscence. These group sessions, as well as conversations with individuals, have been recorded, transcribed and finally edited, to form the verbatim accounts which appear in this book. In some cases it has been necessary to rearrange the material and make slight alterations for the sake of clarity, although we have tried to maintain and safeguard the tone of the original.

While the result is not a comprehensive account of women's war work, it does provide a clear picture of the wide range of jobs which suddenly opened up for women, and of their undoubted skill and ability in these new areas. These individual stories project a positive image of women as flexible and efficient workers, and show how preconceptions about their capabilities were broken down as a consequence of their involvement in the war effort.

An important result of war work for many women was greater financial and personal independence than they had previously known. However, those who took over jobs formerly done by men, often found that their pay and status did not rise accordingly. The campaign for equal pay and opportunities still continues, fifty years later.

Pam Schweitzer

ACKNOWLEDGEMENTS

For general help and advice:
David Strong, Lambeth Libraries
James, Assistant Warden, Thorndike O.P.H.
Mrs. Nell Higgins, Pakeman Day Centre
Fawcett Library, City of London Polytechnic
Wesley Harry, Woolwich Arsenal
The BBC for the loan of a Uher recorder and tapes
Manor House Library, Lewisham
Woodlands History Library, Greenwich
Minet Library, Lambeth

Thingummy-Bob Song, Words and Music by B. Gordon, B. Thomas and D. Heneker (c) 1941,
Reproduced by kind permission of Francis Day and Hunter Ltd., London WC2H 0EA

For allowing us to photographs and other illustrations:
Laurie Dennett, S.T.C.,   T.U.C. Libraries
Wesley Harry, Woolwich Arsenal
The Imperial War Museum (cover photograph)
Margaret Kippin   Patricia Graves
Rose Mullet   Mrs. Wyles
Bill and Joan Welch   Ellen Harbard
Mr. and Mrs. Jones   Daisy Hawkes
Ruth Granville   Dorothy Barton

We wish to thank Helena Platt, the transcribing tapes and P. Graham, for typing and transcripts.

Mrs. Crane

On October 21st, 1940 Mum and I were bombed out. The doctor said that if I hadn't tried so hard to keep calm, I would have been alright, but as it was, I developed a nervous eczema, which I then had for 24 years. He advised me to join the Land Army, rather than the forces, because it would be better for me with my skin problem. So that's why I went into the Land Army.

After being accepted, I waited about a month, then I got a letter saying would I go to Paddington Station and that my gear was coming.

No one gave me a medical, and whether they applied to my doctor I don't know.

My gear arrived and there was much giggling on Mum's and my part. It was strange, because I'd never been away from home, or worn trousers. I'd been brought up to believe that women didn't wear trousers. It was indecent. I only received top gear. All my underwear and everything else I had to find the coupons for. I had to rob Mum of her clothing coupons and take my ration book and registration card with me. Mum was shattered, because one person's rations was very small.

In my family it was always the rule that you had one vest on, one vest off and one in the wash, so I took two vests with me. I took pants, stockings, petticoat, frock, pyjamas, slippers and my kit.

I set off for Paddington, wondering what the heck I'd let myself in for. We reported to Land Army officials, who were women. They were all rather county and jolly hockey sticks, some in uniform, some in plain clothes, with armbands proclaiming they were somebody of importance.

We travelled to Woking on the train with soldiers, but we were carefully segregated. What they thought we'd get up to in front of everybody else I don't know.

When we arrived officials dropped us off at our billets. They'd say: "Here's your two Land Girls and here's their first week's board." Then we were handed what remained of our first week's wages. The wages were 30/- a week and we got half.

My first billet was with a husband and wife called Mr. and Mrs. Bird. He was a burly farm worker and she was small and pecked around like a bird. I shared my room and bed with another land girl called Maude. I was an only child and had never shared a bed with anyone. When I woke up next morning, my nose was rubbing Maude's hair and she was alive with nits. I had to tell her: "I'm sorry Maude, but do you realize that you've got nits?"

I've always sworn that if somebody stood Maude on her head, the nits would have carried her off. Her brown hair was white with nits. Of course, I'd just come from working in a hairdressers salon, and I had no wish to

have those sorts of visitors thank you very much. So I had to go off and get the stuff that night to start cleaning it.

Mr. and Mrs. Bird had to provide us with bed, breakfast, evening meal and sandwiches for mid-day. That depends what you mean by sandwiches. We had four slices of bread, very thinly cut, and she wafted the knife over the margarine, then wafted that onto our bread, slapped a lettuce leaf on the top and if you were very very lucky, she did the same with some fish paste. She made money out of it, because the lettuce was grown in the garden, and the bread was certainly not door steps. The breakfasts were oats boiled in water, so you had a plate of grey nasty water with lumps in, because she could never manage to get the lumps out.

I phoned up the Land Army and said: "Look I want to change my billet. If you want me to stay in the Land Army then you'll let me do this." So I moved round the corner to stay with another woman. There was no gas, no electricity, because her husband didn't believe in new fangled things, and she cooked on an old fashioned range and two Beatrice stoves, but the food was delicious.

My first job was working for a man, who was a threshing contractor. He owned a traction engine and would get hired by farmers to thresh their fields. He would pick Maude and me up at 7 am and take us home in the evening.

On the first day he said to me: "You up there. You do this." Then he got down and left me. I had to catch the sheaves, cut the string and throw them into a big drum. There was no protection from the machinery, and sometimes it was slippery, especially if straw was under your feet. If I got a bundle that was tied wrongly, and I couldn't get it untied, the machine would rise to a high pitched whine. The boss, (never knew his name, just Boss) would get angry because I was losing him money.

If we did barley, the hairs would split and lodge in our feet, behinds, fingers, necks and we had to get them out with a needle, or they'd go septic. It was filthy work. We were black from dust when we got home.

"Boss" used to live in a caravan with his mate, who worked with us. One day Boss said to Maude: "Don't want you here no more." Then he tuned to me and said, "But I'll keep you on. Only I ain't fetching you anymore. You can live in my caravan with us." The caravan was absolutely filthy. He dropped us off and said to me "I'll pick you up in the morning." I thought, "No you won't."

Next morning Maude and I went to the Land Army headquarters in Reading. You should have seen their faces, when we told them. All they said was: "You've got a black mark for refusing to work. Go back to your billet, we'll see about it."

Next week I was sent somewhere else. The farmer was a lay preacher and as mean as muck. We weren't allowed to stop between 7.30 am. when we started till 12.30pm when we had our dinner. Then between 1.30pm till darkness you couldn't stop. If a girl stood up, or went to the loo, she was warned and if she did it again, she had a quarter hour's pay stopped. We were working on a mixed farm, hoeing, planting, and gathering for market. Back-breaking work. I could never understand how he knew someone stood up, until one morning I was told to hoe round the leeks that were near the farm house. I noticed a tiny ridge with a tree on it, and who should be there watching all the girls, but the lay preacher. When he went in for dinner, his sons took over standing by the tree spying on us.

I stayed there for nearly a year and then put in for a transfer.

My next farm was called Speedgate Farm. There were three farms, one for fruit, one for chickens and one dairy farm. I worked on the fruit farm. We called the man who owned it Grandpa. He was more englightened than the others. We were allowed to spend a penny, and have ten minute's break in the morning. There was a thresher, but Grandpa wouldn't let us girls on top, because he thought it was too dangerous.

When we did potato picking, Grandpa put us on piece work. We thought we might earn a bit extra, of course, we never did.

At Speedgate five of us had our own cottage and the farm worker's wife cooked for us. Three of us slept in one room, but we had our own beds. I could bring home five big potatoes, someone else could get six cracked eggs and the dairy girls brought in milk. We helped each other. We'd leave a large kettle of water on the coal range, and when the dairy girls got up, they'd put water on for us. We had a wind-up gramophone and we used to play silly games.

On Friday nights, a car would come for us to take us to the nearest army camp. We always had to wear our breeches, and there was nothing funnier than Land Girls dancing with soldiers with their breeches. The service women never spoke to us. We were ostracized.

Thinking about it, we had a good system at the cottage. I liked mending, so I'd mend socks. Someone else liked cleaning, so she'd do that, someone else was good at cleaning boots. Yes it worked well.

I had to leave that job, because with my eczema I had to go to the hospital every three months and the farm bailiff couldn't stand it.

My next job was looking after vegetables and fruit at Queen Mary's Hospital, Sidcup. We also had to feed the pigs. Never tangle with a pig; it's not worth it. They would find the most ingenious ways of getting out. I spent many a time chasing piglets round the grounds of the hospital. I enjoyed it though.

Looking back on it the Land Army work was hard, dangerous and dirty, but while the men were fighting we were doing what we could. Most of us felt like that. War work certainly made many women independent for the first time. Suddenly you could earn your own money and spend it how you wished. We had more freedom. We could go to the pictures by ourselves, go to dances. A common complaint among women who worked in the Land Army was fibrocytis, or inflammation of the fibres of the back. Many women got invalided out of the Land Army for that. I have it. I've had it for years.

Bridget

I came over here from Ireland for my brother's wedding and I thought to myself, well, it's lovely to be away, and I was to go back the following Monday, but I never did.

The war had just broken out and being a farmer's daughter, land greatly appealed to me. I knew so much about it, cattle and everything, so I joined the Land Army. I was sent to Lincolnshire. It's a real farming place, Lincolnshire.

I was billetted with a particular farmer, there were a few of us, I forget how many now. We lived on the farm with the farmer and his wife and family. They fed us and we were treated like one of the family.

I did everything on the farm from milking, mucking out, to attending a cow who was calving.

One or two of the women were used to farming, but the others used to say to me: It's alright for you, because you can handle the cattle, but we can't. We want to see the back of those cows as soon as we can!"

A job with a farmer is not an easy one, but you have to get on with it. In the mornings it wasn't what time you decide to get up, it was what time you had to get up! I was up at 6.30am. and in between milking the cows in the morning and evening, I'd be digging potatoes and dealing with the hay, corn and barley. I loved it.

We sometimes had nights off, but there was night duty, because if there was a cow in labour you had to help attend that cow all night and you were lucky if you got to sleep for an hour the next day.

I didn't stay in the Land Army for very long, because I was courting. I was already engaged to one chap, but then I met Johnnie. My landlady said to me: "That Johnnie is the man for you!" I finished with the other chap and here I am married forty-three years!

I did enjoy my Land Army work. Sometimes I wish I was back with it, even at the age I am.

AS WE HOPE WE LOOK   AS WE GENERALLY DO LOOK
A sketch by a member of the Women's Land Army, in the 'Land Girl'

The Land Girl's Song

I'm milking – at last I can actually milk
It took me some time, but I stuck it
So now I milk Buttercup, Daisy and Jane
And I really get froth on the bucket!
I think by next week I shall even milk four.
   My word, we are
   Winning the War!

I'm feeding the calves and the pig and the hens
   (Yes, I carefully boil all the swill)
And the cows and the horses, the sheep and
                                      the ducks
Oh, the coupons are tiresome, but still
The hens go on laying, the pigs are
                              eight score
   My word, we are
   Winning the War!

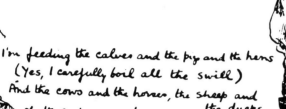

I'm hoeing, my word I should say I can hoe
I've been doing it for weeks and for weeks
My back's used to stooping, but how I do wish
That my blouse wouldn't gap from my breeks!
But the crops are all growing as never before
So what matter – we're Winning the War!

I'm ploughing, my word I should say I can plough
   The tractor is always my choice
I have dragged, drilled and harrowed,
                  disc-harrowed and all
And I sing at the top of my voice
As I swing round the headland and turn up once more
   'My word, we are Winning the War.

'Caveson'

Dorothy

I was born in Deptford, just at the top of Tanners Hill. You can't get any more of a town girl than that!

I was working in a naval outfitters and they were calling up people of seventeen upwards, so I knew I'd have to go. One of my cousins joined the A.T.S. and she hated it. To be honest, I couldn't see myself marching and saluting every Tom, Dick and Harry. So one day I found a recruiting office for the Land Army and on the spur of the moment I joined.

They were appalled that I didn't know one side of a cow from the other, but they still had me. They were desperate for dairy girls, so they put me down for that.

I went to be trained for a month at Sevenoaks. We were in a big house with a senior girl, one under her, and a woman who cooked and cleaned.

When we arrived, no one knew anything about cows, so they rigged up an apparatus, like a rubber glove with teats, and we had to practice on that. You can imagine the hilarity that went on squirting it around!

At 9 o'clock, the head girl said: "It's time for bed. You have to got to bed early, because you get up early, at 4am." We thought she was joking and we all went to bed laughing, but at 4am next morning we were all routed out of bed.

I'll never forget, till my dying day, that first morning. Four o'clock in February, out of bed, downstairs, a thick door-step of bread and jam, a cup of tea, and then a mile walk to the farm. We had to be there at five o'clock, and anybody who was late had to walk along eating their bread and jam.

We were shown how to clean the cows and wash their udders, and then we were actually shown how to milk. After watching a few times, we were given a cow, and we had to sit down and do it. Nobody told us, but cows don't like new people, and they hold back their milk.

After about twenty minutes, I'd got about a teaspoon full in my bucket. The senior girl came up to me, and she said, "You've got some then." Then she said, "Get up," and she gave the cow a thump with her first, and said, "Let it go, you bugger!", and in about two seconds flat she had a bucket full of frothy milk. I looked at her, and she laughed and said, "They always do that when you're new."

About the second morning, they were letting it go and you could get a fair amount. One of the young men or the girls would come and finish off. By the end of the week you were milking like old hands. Then we had to learn to bottle the milk, and that was terribly cold. The milk used to go through various instruments and gadgets, with cold water flowing through it. When it came to the bottling, all the cold, ice cold milk was running all over your hands. Just imagine that at 7 o'clock on a cold morning. We had to bottle them and top them, and put them in racks.

Then we went home to breakfast, and after that we had to walk back to the farm, where we learned how to clean out the cow shed and wash and sterilize all the equipment that had been used in the milking. Then we walked back and had a big dinner. As soon as we'd finished eating, we all rushed upstairs and fell on our beds for a couple of hours. Then we all walked back to the farm again for the afternoon milking, which was the

same as the morning.

We didn't have time to look at the country. We went out at half past four in the morning, and we didn't get back till half past six at night, so it was pitch-black. We were there for a month, and I suppose they though if we could cope with that month we could cope with anything. It really was hard. When we had finished our training we were sent home to wait to be allocated a farm to work on.

First of all I went to a temporary one, and it turned out to be very temporary! It was in Essex somewhere, so it was a long journey, and the farmer took one look at me and said, "Oh no dear, I want someone a bit tougher." I was humiliated. I got there on a Saturday, and he couldn't send me home on a Sunday, because he couldn't get through to the Land Army, so on Monday morning, he rang to say could I be replaced. They sent me out to round up the cows. I suppose they thought, well, at least she can do that. So I went out in my new clothes, all spotlessly clean, and I was trampling around this flat marshy field, calling the cows, when I put my foot in a hole I hadn't seen. I lost my balance, slipped over and lost a wellington, and went head first into this quagmire. I walked back to the farm, with my welly boot in my hand, trying hard not to cry. I was terribly depressed, minus the cows. The farmer's wife just looked at me, as if she'd never seen anything like it in her life. He rang the Land Army on Monday, and said he didn't think I was strong enough for his farm, and could they send him a bigger, tougher girl.

My next job was a permanent one. Another Land Girl and I were stationed on a farm near Tunbridge Wells.

We lived in the top half of a farm house, and the cowman and his wife lived underneath. Because there was no electricity, and only two rooms were furnished, we thought we'd sleep in the same room. We were glad we did afterwards, because the cowman was very peculiar.

He used to knock at our windows late at night, and we were afraid that he had a key, so we had the boy, who worked on the farm, fit a bolt to the inside of our bedroom door.

One night he knocked on our window with a stick and said that the cows had got out we had to get up. It was 2am and there we were on our bikes, and him walking, looking for these dratted cows. Later my friend said: "Damn it, I'm going back." We went back and being on our bikes we didn't care and we left him ranting and raving behind us. Later on when we got up, the cows were in their field, they hadn't got out at all.

He never tried anything on me, but I think he must have done with the other girl, because one weekend, I came back, and found the front door locked. I had to throw stones at the window until she let me in. She said: "Don't take your coat off, we're going to see the farmer." The farmer told us that he'd like to dismiss the cowman, but he didn't think we could run the farm by ourselves, so because my friend was leaving, I had to as well. She never did tell me what went on.

Then I went to another place, West Malling, in Kent, for another temporary job, but I decided that I was a bit fed up with milking. It was so boring, the same old thing all the time. We never saw anything or did anything, so I asked if I could be transferred to something else. They wrote to say that they were opening a new hostel in Lenham, Kent, and they had hand-picked twelve land girls to go there, so I went. We had a huge house on the edge of the village, set in its own grounds, and I had to work on a farm in the village. I spent two of the happiest years of my life there. I worked with an old man and two horses. He was a marvellous old man. He must have been in his seventies then, and he taught me how to work with these horses, and harness and handle them. They were shire horses, enormous things, and I was terrified when I first saw them, but they were very easy to handle. After about two years, the farmer left, and the new man didn't want horses, so the old man I worked with decided to retire. The horses were going, so we were going. I still lived at the hostel, and I had to go out and work with the girls who were in gangs, picking potatoes, cutting cabbages, and clearing the apple orchards so that they could be re-ploughed.

At Lenham the people were very suspicious, because they'd never had land girls in the area before. I think they saw the hostel as a den of iniquity, with all the girls from London coming in. That was why all the first girls were hand-picked. We were all very similar types, a bit staid, and loners.

Our Matron, at the hostel, was a marvellous woman. She looked exactly like an elderly spinster, although she wasn't that old. When the soldiers used to take a girl out, Matron would insist that they came to the hostel and knocked for the girl. She'd open the door and inspect the fellow, ask him who he'd come to see, sit him down in the hall and bellow the girl's name at the top of her voice. She used to say that she wanted to see who her girls were going out with. At night we had to be in at ten o'clock, to be up early for work. Matron used to stand at the front door, and bang a wooden spoon on a frying pan to call us in. You could hear it a mile and a half away.

Nobody ordered you about in the Land Army. If they did, and you didn't want to do it, then you didn't do it. On the whole we kept to our uniform, because we were quite proud of it, but people wore their hats in funny ways, to have some individuality, and to show that they didn't have to do as they were told.

We were proud of being Land Girls, and we were fed up when we didn't get the recognition we thought we ought we ought to have. After all, we did a lot more than a lot of girls in the armed forces. If it hadn't been for us, a lot of the people wouldn't have eaten. We got no recognition at the end of the war. In the Victory Parade at Maidstone, they put us behind the boy scouts, until we complained. The army was shattered: they didn't know what to do with this kind of insubordination, but we were quite determined. If they didn't put us somewhere else, we were going to go home. In the end they put us behind the ATS, so that was all right. We marched in step with them.

When I came out of the Land Army I sent my uniform back, and I got a few pages of clothing coupons in exchange. That was all. I didn't have enough to buy new clothes. I really hated coming back. I was quite happy to be home again, but life seemed so aimless. For years I didn't know what to do with myself. I just wandered about at weekends, and I had a terrible job to find work I really liked. I'd lost my typing speed, although I was still all right on figures. I took a job at the United Dairies depot, checking the milk men's round books, for the sake of getting experience, and then I went into a typing pool at Woolwich. That was sheer hell, and I didn't stay there long. As I got one or two more jobs, I got more experience, and in the end I went back up to into town and got a job there.

It was a terrible wrench. I felt as if I'd lost something, lost part of me. Part of me was still in the country. A friend and I used to go on farming holidays, with the forestry commission. We'd set out in gangs by the lorry load and work in the fields, as we had done in the Land Army. It was more for fun and company than anything else. I don't honestly think I've met a land girl who didn't enjoy her work. There's something about being out in the open air. It was odd really, for a girl from Depford, but I was mad keen.

Valerie

I went away to university when I was seventeen, the University of Wales, at Aberystwyth. During the long vacations the NUS asked people to go and help with the Land Army. I thought it would be a nice outdoor life, so I put my name down and I was selected to go. I was sent a travel voucher, and I caught the train at Newport with one other student from Aberystwyth. We went on the

train from Bristol to Barnstable, where we'd been given instructions to wait on the platform. We were picked up by a farm lorry and taken to a place called Saunton, outside the village of Braunton, on Saunton Sands, which is on the North Coast of Devon. By this time we were quite a large party, of about twenty or twenty-five. We were taken to an hotel which had been requisitioned.

We were all allocated to farms in the district. In the one I was chosen to go to, which was a market garden farm, there were two land girls, plus a foreman. We were divided into groups and we had one land girl in charge of our group, and the other one was in charge of the other group. When we were picked up in the morning they came with us. Then we worked alongside them, and they were in charge of us. The lorry came to fetch us at seven in the morning. We were called at about six, and then we had breakfast. We started work at half past seven, and then at half past nine we had a break, when we used to eat something to have a cup of tea or some other drink. You just sat down on the spot, wherever you were. The farm was given over mostly to tomato growing. First thing in the morning we had to work inside the glass houses, because it got too hot later on. We used to go along picking the very tiny tomatoes that were not good for the plant and also weren't good enough to be sold. That was a nice little perk, because we were allowed to eat those ourselves. Also we were trained to pluck out any small growths between the joints in the tomato plants. From about elven o'clock on we moved out into the fields, and we did the same there. Sometimes we'd get sent to do the celery. That was awful, because at a certain point in the growth of celery it has to be hoed up to stop it from getting green, and you had to do this on your hands and knees, by hand. Some people were unfortunate enough to be put on the potato raising. That was really back-breaking stuff. We also did pea picking. It was very tedious, but we chatted away

like mad and gossipped and sang. The foreman used to come round and get irate with us sometimes, but on the whole he was alright, very pleasant.

We used to finish at about half past four. The lorry'd come and collect us again, and it'd tear along the country lanes back to the hostel. One of the hotels still had a bar open, so we used to go there in the evenings sometimes. We weren't allowed on the beach because it was mined, although one part of it was left open, and we used to have a bathe. The whole place was crawling with armed forces of various nationalities, because it was very near to RAF Chiverton, one of the big aerodromes. There used to be dances on a Wednesday in Braunton, and also on a Saturday, so we used to cycle in and go to them. There were organisations like the WVS arranging them, and we would be invited. Obviously they wanted girls to go, otherwise it wouldn't be much fun for the forces. You got to know a little group of people, and actually I met some quite nice blokes. One was an American air force fellow who was extremely pleasant. One night he came and he'd brought a whole stack of chocolate and nylons, and he said he was awfully sorry, but he was going the following day, and would I like these, because I reminded him of his sister. I do remember one occasion, though, when I felt very unsafe indeed. We were asked to make up a party, myself and one of the girls who shared my room. We went down onto the burrows, and there were two of us and four of these Americans, and I remember thinking, 'My God, we're in trouble'. But we kept talking; it was like a kind of instinct. One of them was a very decent guy, older than the rest, and I think we got away with it because of that. Quite honestly, I think it was a very near thing. The really dangerous ones, though, were the Poles! You didn't go anywhere by yourself with the Poles if you could help it. They were very pleasant, and terribly chivalrous and glamorous, full of gold teeth and braid and all the rest of it, but all they wanted to do was get you behind a hedge. I remember going to Barnstable on a Saturday off, and two Poles attached themselves to us. We really got fed up with them, and so we proceeded to speak entirely in Welsh, which neither of us could really speak. We recited the whole of the Lord's Prayer in Welsh to each other, talking a line at a time, and various things like the national anthem, so that it sounded like conversation. They didn't know what nationality we were, and we made them keep on guessing, but of course, they never guessed. In the end they gave up. They realised we were having them on, and they went off.

The day the war ended I was out rowing in Cardigan Bay. It was the most beautiful day. We'd already heard that it was on the point of finishing, and there was tremendous euphoria. The war was a very peculiar thing: the whole world was like a melting pot. I was in a back water most of the time, but you knew so many people who were killed or disappeared, or were maimed, or became prisoners of war. Every family had somebody. Although I in fact wasn't in much mortal danger, you never knew what is going to happen. There was this terrible feeling of uneasiness and insecurity. You didn't know whether life was going to go on.

Prim

I was an invoice clerk an exporting firm and they had managed to get me exempt from being called up several times.

When I was twenty eight and a half I did, however, get nabbed. I went for the interview and I remember the woman looking at my date of birth and saying: "Oh dear, you're too old for the forces, you'd best go in the N.A.A.F.I." I'm not going there I thought!

I'd been "genned up" about the Women's Timber Corps by my brother, and being with the Woodcraft Folk, I had experience of camping. So I told her that I would do that. "What makes you think you're strong enough?" was her reply. But I went for the medical anyway.

The medical was ever so strict. The way he examined me! I had to take all my clothes off and he asked if my heart was good, my feet, ears, head, everything. I sent my medical form off and I received a reply telling me to report at Bury St Edmunds.

At Bury St. Edmunds we received our kit. All I had to bring was my washing tackle and pyjamas. We were stationed in an old army camp in three huts. There were twelve of us in each hut, with fires each end and nice beds, toilets and showers. The food was fantastic and we got a damn good breakfast.

The first day we went out to the forest and we were given these big axes. Some of the girls were only nineteen and had never seen an axe in their lives. I don't know why they volunteered. Anyway the man in charge showed us this piece of wood. He went chop, chop, chop and the most wonderful V appeared on his piece of wood. Then it was our turn! Well, you can imagine. The axes went all over the place. At least I'd been to camp, so I could chop a piece of wood, not perfect, but not too bad. Our first axe was not sharp, as he said: "I don't want you chopping your legs off." Our second was better though, so we could make decent grooves in the wood. We practised all day long with the logs. It was great.

The next day he said: "Now we're going to fell a tree, so I need a girl to help me."

They both knelt either side of this tree and went in a little way with the saw. Then with his axe, he went down right into the cut that had been made and kept hitting the tree. Then both of them went round the back with the saw.

He then said: "Now listen girls, this is the most important thing. Pick that saw up otherwise it will fly back when the tree falls and it will hurt you badly. Then look round, see there's no-one in your way, and shout "Timber" and push the tree."

Then it was our turn to try. The worst bit was actually carrying the brush over to the bonfire. Being in the Woodcraft Folk, I knew that if I put two fairly large bits of brush down and stacked the wood across and used a piece of string, we could drag it. Well everyone then did the same thing.

We learned how to make pit props to go down the mines and how to scrape away the bark of thin trees to make telegraph poles. That was a messy jogb, because all the sap stuck to your dungarees. I made sure I didn't do too many of them!

After our month's training we had another medical. A girl I was friendly with failed, because she had flat feet. Why she couldn't chop down trees with flat feet I don't know. Anyway I was sent to a saw mill, and found myself at Downtown near Salisbury.

Another girl and I got billetted with a woman and her child. We got 50/- a week, but had to give up our wages to her, and she gave us 14/- a week pocket money. Later a man at the saw mill told us that if we joined the union, we'd get better pay. When we did join, we didn't tell her and kept the extra to ourselves.

This woman we were with never did our washing. At first we tried to do it, but we were so short of gear that I used to send our washing home to my Mum. We'd send it on Saturday and she'd get it on Monday and do it on the same day and return it. There'd always be a bar of chocolate or something in it. She was a brick my Mum.

Our kit consisted of two pairs of breeches, mine were grey velvet, very posh. Three fawn shirts, a green pullover, two pairs of overalls, two pairs of dungarees, long fawn socks, brown shoes, two pairs of boots, one mackintosh, one overcoat, and other bits and pieces. These were expected to last at least a year, but the socks wore out ever so quickly. We also had our Timber Corps badges and our beret hats, not the Land Army hats.

The hours we worked weren't bad. We'd start at about 8am. and it depended how light it was when we finished. Our saw mill had a roof on it, but all the sides were open and the wood was in the open air.

The first month was pretty grim, because Mr Mitchell, the owner, hadn't provided for us girls. We went to the toilet in pairs to keep watch, because there was only an Elsan toilet and that was a man's.

When the welfare officer came and we told her, she said: "Oh, I can't have that. These girls must have their own room where they can have their own Elsan and also where they can boil a kettle and have a hot drink. Also I want a man put in charge of the toilet, so when it's full he can empty it." That's when we got George. He was a nice little man, the littlest man in the saw mill. We used to play cards with George in his house. He used to keep a pig and have it killed and keep another and he kept them as clean as a new pin. He gave up his meat ration, so he could keep them. Nice was George. Real country bloke.

We did all sorts of jobs at the saw mill, delivering firewood, loading wood onto trains, making struts for ceilings and I did coffin wood.

Coffin wood was elm. We had this big circular saw and when it started to cut through the tree, I would run round and hammer in a pointed wooden marker on each side, otherwise the saw would have made a mark in the wood. When we'd finished, the whole trunk would be in six foot pieces with these markers in it.

When you did coffin wood and the saw hit a knot, or a bullet, you had to change the saw. To do this, the man in charge would loosen the saw, pinch one end of it together and call me over. I'd get the pinched end and, holding it, put it on my head and he'd to the same with his end. Off we'd go to the saw doctor. The saw was over six feet wide, so when we carried it we'd shout: Beware, saw!" Everyone would get out of the way!

After we'd been there sometime, Mr Mitchell told us that he had to take in Italian prisoners, but that we were not to speak to them. We got paired off with them to work. I was paired with Rob and he could speak good English. Imagine not being supposed to speak to him!

Well, Mr Mitchell's uncle came to the mill one day and said that he was going to put Rob on four by fours. He looked at Rob then said: "Four by four" and showed his fingers. He then got a ruler and counted very slowly "One, two, three, four". He then got a piece of wood and said: "I show." He did it and then said: "You comprit, understand, comprit." Rob looked at him and said: "No."

Mr Mitchell's uncle had to do it all over again. When he'd gone, Rob in perfect English mimicked him. I was in hysterics. The uncle comes rushing back: "What's the matter? What's the matter?" Well, I couldn't tell him, so I said: "I don't think he understands you." Well, the uncle did it all over again.

When the other girl I shared my billet with and I went to Salisbury on Saturdays, we'd sometimes see the Italian prisoners walking about. You couldn't mistake them, because they had those horrible orangey suits with big patches on them.

The woman we stayed with was possessive and didn't like us going out on Saturday or Sunday. She wanted us to stay with her, so we'd tear home on Saturday after work, have lunch and cycle into Salisbury. We'd have early tea at the Cadena and then go to the services theatre to see a play. James Mason was in the audience once. We had to wear our Timber Corps uniforms otherwise we wouldn't get in. When the Americans arrived, some of them must have complained, that they couldn't get in or something, because one week there was a notice up saying we couldn't get in. The soldiers were so annoyed, because they used to take friends in, that they refused to go, so in the end the notice was taken down.

On Sundays my friend and I would tell our landlady that we didn't want any breakfast, and we'd cycle to this smashing little place where we'd get breakfast. We even went to the Isle of Wight once. I was a bit old for cycling then, so that trip tired me out.

We worked really hard in the Timber Corps. One year it was a really bad winter, lots of snow and only two men turned up for work. We girls used the electric saws and cut up timber in the yard. The next day, when the men came they were amazed and wanted to know how the wood got cut. They couldn't believe that we turned up in the snow.

I remember one night we'd been at George's and he kept us late and said: "I suppose you want some supper." So we had bacon sandwiches with onions he kept for years. Well, we had this and we were late leaving and we were just getting past the hill, when suddenly men jumped out at us saying: "Halt who goes there?" It was the men from the mill... They recognised us, but were fooling around and told us to hurry home, or we'd get pelted with soot and flour. Sure enough we just got in, when there was this riot outside and they were having a mock battle. They were in the Home Guard and they were having a mock battle with soot and flour.

They took it seriously!

After I did my three years service, the export business was picking up again, so I asked the firm to get me

HOME TIMBER PRODUCTION DEPARTMENT
MINISTRY OF SUPPLY

WOMEN'S TIMBER CORPS

First and foremost I send to all members of the Women's Timber Corps in England and Wales, our very best wishes from Headquarters for 1943. When the Timber Corps was established in April we inherited 1,000 Land Army volunteers who had already been giving good services to the Department. They formed the nucleus of our Corps and we are grateful to them for giving us such a good foundation. Since April our numbers have risen over the 3,000 mark and the range of our work has been progressively widened. As more young men have to be called to the Forces, the Women's Timber Corps must play a still bigger part in production through the critical offensive year of 1943. Timber is one of the bulkiest imports, the more timber you produce or help to produce, the more ships are released for the offensive. During 1942 some workers in the Women's Timber Corps were saving shipping space at the rate of 50 tons per year each.

THE LAND GIRL

| No. 8, Volume 4 | NOVEMBER, 1943 | Price 3d. |

released. I loved my job as an invoice clerk and never wanted to do war work. All the time I was in the Timber Corps, I was homesick. The firm managed to get me a quick release.

The war was a good time for women getting on. It certainly made me stronger. When I was told that I was going back to my job, Miss Maisie told me that I should not go back for £3 a week, but to ask for more.

When I went to see the boss, and he said how happy he was that he had got me released and that I would get £3 a week, I said: "No." He was shocked and then said: "Well, what about £3/10- or £4" I said: "Yes, alright." Then I went back. Before the war I never would have done that!

We Timber Corps girls were snooty. We thought that we were better than the Land Girls, because we worked harder and we got more pay!

WOMEN'S LAND ARMY (ENGLAND AND WALES).
RELEASE CERTIFICATE.

The Women's Land Army for England and Wales acknowledges with appreciation the services given by

Miss D. G. Hawkes.

who has been an enrolled member for the period from

15th February 1943. to *13th February* 1946.

and has this day been granted a willing release.

Date *14th February, 1946.* *MeeBaw*

COUNTY SECRETARY, WOMEN'S LAND ARMY.

Telephone : Lyndhurst 318.

Any further communication on this subject should be addressed to THE DIVISIONAL OFFICER, and the following number quoted.

File I.307.

Your Ref.

MINISTRY OF SUPPLY,
HOME TIMBER
PRODUCTION DEPARTMENT,
No. 6 DIVISION,
RED LODGE,
LYNDHURST, HANTS.

February 9th.,1946.

Miss D. Hawkes,
C/o Mrs Mitchener,
9, Vale Road,
Woodfalls,
Nr. Salisbury,
Wilts.

Dear Miss Hawkes,

The National Service Officer has now given permission for your release from the Timber Corps of the Women's Land Army. The Land Army Authorities are being notified to this effect and you will receive in due course a formal letter of discharge from that body.

Your Land Army uniform, also your Timber Corps Beret and Badge must now be returned to the The Uniform Dept., Ministry of Supply, H.T.P.D. Vassall Road, Fishponds, Bristol. You may, however, keep your shoes, shirts, stockings and overcoat if you have further need of them. On receipt of this uniform any refund of coupons due to you will made. Your rubber boots and/or forestry cycle should be handed in to your employer before you leave.

I should like to take this opportunity of thanking you for all the good work which you have done whilst in the Timber Corps and I wish you every success and happiness for the future.

Good Luck,

Yours sincerely,

R. K. Coombes.

Welfare Officer 6.

JOIN THE ATS

ASK FOR INFORMATION AT THE NEAREST EMPLOYMENT EXCHANGE OR AT ANY ARMY OR ATS RECRUITING CENTRE

I came from Austria. I came here before the war in 1939. Hitler had already moved into Austria, and the rumour was that he would marry all the young girls off to the Nazis to get children. I wasn't married then, so I wanted to get out quick.

The only person, who knew I wanted to go to England was my mother. I didn't trust anyone. You couldn't even trust your own people. If they had said just one word, the Nazis would have found out that I wanted to get out because of Hitler. They would have put me in the labour camps. I kept it secret, and when I knew everything was ready, I told my family. They could hardly believe it.

You had to have a visa to leave. The authorites asked me millions of questions, and I said that I was going as a domestic help to an English family. That was allowed at the time. That's how I got out; otherwise I don't think I could have.

A whole lot of the girls were Jewish, and they had to get leave to come to England. Men couldn't go out at all. In Cologne they took the Jewish girls off the train, stripped them naked and searched them for jewellery before we passed over to Holland. I got through easily, because I wasn't Jewish. Getting to England was like heaven.

I worked as a domestic help for two years. There were four of us with that family. We lived in. There was a parlourmaid, a cook, the children's nurse, and a chauffeur. They could all join the army, so those rich people were lumbered. Not being British, I couldn't join up straight away, so I had to take all the work over from the others who had left. I never had a day off.

Then I heard that I could join up, so I volunteered because I wanted to do something to help against Hitler. I never had a chance to join the WAAF, because I wasn't English. They took the better girls in the WAAF, better educated. We were lucky they took us anyway, because there were only a few of us left. The others were all interned.

I was in the A.T.S., for four and a half years. I got paid 11/-a week, with the food and lodging and clothes. We were very poor in the army. I was attached to the Royal Engineers and they moved you from one place to another. I just did catering. That's all I was allowed to do, because I was not English. I was in the driver's training camp. We had three thousands boys there. My friend was the cook and we were in the kitchen serving. It was very hard work. I never worked so hard in my life, but I enjoyed myself. We had plenty to eat.

 IMPORTANT

Government Announcement to Women

Ministry of Labour and National Service

There must no longer be any doubt in anybody's mind that every available woman in Britain will have to serve to win this war.

The Registration of age groups will proceed steadily. But this process, which necessarily involves interviewing, takes up precious time, and thousands of volunteers are needed at this moment in the A.T.S. for work that cannot wait. In the hour of their country's need, the Women of Britain have always responded, unselfishly and most courageously, to the call for service. The hour of need is upon us now.

You are being asked to volunteer to-day ahead of your age group. If you have already registered do not wait for your interview. Come forward, and say you want to help now.

There are many different ways in which you can serve, but the need of the AUXILIARY TERRITORIAL SERVICE is very great indeed. This service demands personal integrity, good intelligence and willingness to maintain a high standard of efficiency.

Members of the A.T.S. are working side by side with men in the Army and are also taking over vital work which releases men for the front line. Come forward now and help to build the mighty army that will lead a great country to Victory.

Post this to-day

Address it to The Auxiliary Territorial Service, AG18/99A, Hobart House, Grosvenor Gardens, London, S.W.1.
Please send me full story of life in the A.T.S. and details of the opportunities it offers. This does not commit me in any way.

Mrs/Miss_____ Age_____
(in confidence)

Address _____

Age limits, 17½ to 43
(Parents' consent needed under 18) Ex-Service women may volunteer up to 50
(Unsealed envelope, penny stamp)

★ Please call and have a talk at any Employment Exchange or A.T.S. or Army Recruiting Centre. They are there to help you.

200,000 ATS urgently needed

12

We had a lovely uniform. It was khaki with a little porridge hat. It was very nice, but the shoes killed me. My feet are crippled from those shoes. They were flat, but the leather was so hard. We had thick coarse stockings, but in the end they let us buy nylon ones, when the nylon came out. We could wear them when we were off duty, but not on duty.

When we were off duty, I was so tired I just fell into bed. I didn't like pubs at all. I used to go with my boyfriend, but I was so tired I would rather go home to bed and sleep. The girls slept in nissan huts. Nissan huts were round iron buildings. They were very nice inside. We had nice beds, nice cupboards, a big oven in the middle, because it was ever so cold in the winter. It was very hot in the summer and very cold in the winter. We had a sitting room, a shower and bathroom. Every day we had a bath. We had to. When you go on duty in the kitchens and work as hard as I did, you look forward to a bath. We went in three at a time. We were sick of queueing!

In some places the local people did treat us alright, but in others they were all stuck up; rich farmers, who didn't want us there at all. In Chesterfield the locals were alright, because they had English, Americans, Indians, Ghurkas, all mixed up there. It was like a garrison town, all the army there. We got lots of lifts from people, when we wanted to go into town. We used to go dancing at R.A.F. camps, and that's where I met my husband. The R.A.F. women never mingled with us. They were jealous of us. They hated us when we came to the camp. You see, they worked there with their men. They knew them. But when new girls came to the camp, of course, the men went after the new girls.

It wasn't fair, the reputation the ATS got. I never went out a lot with boys. We girls went out together, and

when I met my husband I went out with him. In my company I can only remember one girl, who got pregnant, only one. It was a big camp and she left the army before we got demobbed. We didn't say anything: we treated it as nothing special. We were sorry for her really. The father was married.

There were about twenty of us from Austria, and there were Scottish girls, Irish girls, and some from the north. I don't know if it was their first job, but I guess it would be, because they were rather young, about nineteen or twenty.

The women officers were friendly to us, but they weren't allowed to mix. The officers kept to themselves. That's the rule in the army. Some of the women in charge of us were very good. Some were sharp with us, but we got over that. When they trained us they had to be a bit commanding.

I got letters from my family in Vienna, but all censored. They had a terrible time. I lost both my parents. I never saw them again.

" *Tell me, are the women's services the proper place for a nice girl?* "

WHAT THEY DO AND WHAT THEY WEAR...

THE AUXILIARY TERRITORIAL SERVICE

The A.T.S. has been in existence since September 1938. They are doing hundreds of vital jobs, and so releasing more men for other duties. In this capacity the girls are trained as drivers, motor - cycle messengers, draughts-women, cooks, teleprinter operators, and as instrument operators locating the targets for A.A. guns. The Director herself had a hand in the design of the smart, workmanlike A.T.S. uniform. It consists of a simply cut square-shouldered tunic and slim-fitting skirt. The unbelted great-coat fits snugly to the waist. Off duty they wear a smart field-service cap in chocolate and beech brown and leaf green.

WHETHER the job you're doing is in or out of uniform, whether you serve in a factory, an office, a shop or in a home, you'll value the renewed vigour that comes with Personal Freshness for both work and recreation. So it's well worth remembering that Personal Freshness can be renewed simply and daily by the regular use of

LIFEBUOY TOILET SOAP

Sam

I was on the Ack-ack guns. They had ATS women on command posts there. They were plotting where the planes were coming in. They were a blimmin' nuisance to us. You couldn't swear or nothing, and there was a lot of swearing going on in there of course. They used to report us for swearing. They'd say: "Why don't you bag up swearing, Sam." I used to swear and say, "Bugger off out of it." I had no time for them. They were good at their job; I'll tell you that.

SERVE IN THE WAAF
WITH THE MEN WHO FLY

Mrs. Gange

I had been a GPO telephonist before the war. We were living in Sussex. My brother was already in the air force, and I longed to join up. I always longed to do a service for somebody, and I thought I could serve my country if I joined up. I knew it would be a disciplined life, but I liked discipline. My brother agreed with me, but mother wouldn't let me go. I talked it over with my gran, who was always on my side, and she said, "You go, duck, if you want to. I'll see to your mother when you've gone." So, unbeknown to her, I made my way up to Adastral House in London. I told mother I was going to Haywards Heath, caught the train to London, and went for the interview and medical. You had to be A1 to go in. After I'd had the interview they told me that the only jobs that were open were for cooks and waitresses. I said "No thank you, I'll wait until you've got other vacancies." They thought I was was being snobbish, and they asked what qualifications I had. As soon as I said I was a GPO trained telephonist, they said, "Right, you're in," because they were desperate for signals people. They said, "Go back home, and you'll be hearing from us in a few days."

I still said nothing to my mother. I didn't like decieving her. One morning the village Postmaster knocked at the door with a telegram. It said, "You have been accepted," and I had to report on the following Monday at such and such a time. Of course, mother got all worried because of the telegram. She asked me what it was all about, and when I told her she went off at the deep end. We had a tearful goodbye. She broke down and made me cry, but I didn't let her see me. I waited until I got on the bus.

I had to bring a change of underclothes, a set of nightclothes and toiletries. Also I had to take the telegram, my birth certificate and some other means of identification. When I got to Adastral House, we waited about an hour and then we all got marshalled outside. There was this great big truck, open at the back, with benches, and this took us all the way to Gloucester, by road. I was comforting a little seventeen year old, from Scotland. She'd never been away from home before, and she was crying her eyes out. I said, "Go on, have a good cry, if that's what you feel like." I was making them laugh, she and another couple, 'cos I was saying to her, "Just imagine what our mothers would do if they could see us now, sitting in the back of this lorry!" We didn't see much of the countryside, just sitting on two benches, holding on for grim death going round corners, with only the tail-board up at the back.

There were about twenty five of us; that was the London intake. We were taken to Innsworth Court, the recruitment camp. When we rolled up we were all tired. They took us straight to the cookhouse, and as soon as we had a meal we were shown to our quarters, a nissen hut with a funny old stove in the middle of it. At home I'd always had a light at night. I used to sleep in grandma's room, and as soon as that light went out, I'd sit up in the bed gasping for breath. I think it was a fear of blindness, because grandma was going blind. Well, I was scared to death to tell anyone that at twenty years old I had to have a light at night, so I just sat up in bed with my hands round my knees. Half an hour after lights out, the WAAF Flight Sergeant came into the hut, and she said, "What are you girls doing with these blackouts like this. Let the air get in the room. Take those blackouts down." Once those blackouts were down, and I could see the moon, I don't remember going to sleep. A couple of nights like that broke the habit of twenty years.

We got up at about 6.30. We had to troop over to have a wash, and then we had to go before the officer to be sworn in. You had to swear to abide by the Secrecy Act, and after that we had to sign something. Then we went straight to the clothing store to get our uniforms and our other gear. They were all standing behind the counter, and they looked you up and down. We had good uniforms, compared with the men. Also you got towels; you got three pairs of "blackouts", which were knickers; three pairs of "twilights", grey silk knickers, four pairs of grey stockings, and a tie hat. We had two sets of uniform. They were both the same, but one was for parade. We had a respirator, a helmet, which we had to carry everywhere we went, a gas cape, gas goggles, and two pairs of pyjamas, and a great coat. Your hair had to be just so: we had to put a bootlace round our head and roll all our hair into it. It had to be two inches off your collar, and you were put on a charge if it touched. Then we had to go before the officer again, and she told us how to salute. I'll always remember, the first day I went out on the town, I saw this man coming towards me with gold braid all round the peak of his cap, and as he came towards me my knees were knocking. He was the first officer I'd seen. I saluted, and he looked at me in bewilderment and saluted back. He turned round, and he was laughing all over his face. He said, "You'll have to be careful, my dear; there's plenty of us knocking round Gloucester." He was an Electric Light Company inspector!

The initial training was about 4 weeks long, and it really was training. We had to get up every morning, you had an inspection before breakfast. You all lined up outside, in the cold. The Corporal and the Sergeant used to come along with the WAAF Officer and they would inspect you, to see all your buttons were clean, and your shoes and everything. They picked on every little thing they could. Then we went in and had breakfast. After

that, for 1½ hours solid, we went out on the square. It had a flag pole up one end of it, with a flag on. We had an Army Sergeant Major drilling us and he had us marching up and down — left, right, left, right and all the rest of it. If you did anything wrong and he was displeased, he put you on orders, and you might have to go out on the square in the evening for an hour, running up and down, round and round — however long he told you. But they taught you all the elements of drill, and dressing, slow marches for funerals, things like that. I liked it. I had always liked physical exercises at school, so I didn't mind it, that's what we were there to do and we just accepted it.

When it came to leaving, you had an individual interview with the commanding officer. Because we were women we were allowed to pick where we wanted to go. I wanted to get near home, because of getting home on leaves, so I asked to go to Gatwick. I didn't know it was a non-operational station, and she said, "You can't go to Gatwick. Anywhere else?" She showed me the map, and I said, "Oh, Biggih Hill: that's not many miles from where I was born."

As soon as I got there, I had to go and see the signals operator, as I was GPO trained. He said, "You will be a great asset to our troop." Within about a month I was one of the first Leading Air Craft Women, which meant I could have propellor badge on my arm. It's the equivalent to one stripe in the army. It meant an extra shilling a week,

BIGGIN HILL. 1940.

I do my duty every day, I'm a plugger up of calls –
I sit at the board and push my plugs in all the little holes.
Group Captains, Pilots all come up to hear me speak my mind,
And if I hand wrong numbers out, tis then they start to "bind".

It's "Have you got my number Miss? For goodness sake be quick –
I'ts strictly a Priority Call of Course" – that man I'd like to kick –
For after having cut off calls in order to do his bidding,
His opening words are "Hallo my Sweet", I know then he's been kidding.

And then we have the AC plonks, 'browned off' and feeling 'brassed'
Who flash receivers up and down, or forget what calls they've passed.
Or else while I'm connecting calls in high pitched voice they shriek
About their latest conquests, in tones by no means meek.

Then N.C.O's who long ago should have had their discharge papers,
Come on the line and shout and rave and cut all sorts of capers,
They seem to think that a couple of 'tapes' gives them the right to bellow–
What they think of me and the GPO to every WAAF and fellow.

So the next time you pick up the phone and have to wait at all –
Just think of me, the little WAAF, who plugs in all the holes,
Don't think I'm knitting 'comforts' or drinking canteen tea.
For if you could but see me I'm as busy as can be.

MYSELF & PAT CRISP

15

BARBARA (TANKS) MAP WRITER

and of course responsibility. Within a month of that, the corporal in charge of the exchange was posted to another station. The signals operator brought me into his office, and he said, "Well, Cunningham, the corporal has gone. Do you feel capable of taking over the Exchange?" I said "Yes." I thought, anything for a laugh!

I was strict but I was fair when I was doing my work. We were the first ones to get the air raid warnings, and we used to have to give out the warning to the fire

WHAT THEY DO AND WHAT THEY WEAR...

WOMEN'S AUXILIARY AIR FORCE

The Women's Auxiliary Air Force was formed in 1939. Before that members did duty with the Royal Air Force Companies of the A.T.S., formed in 1938. But experience of the specialised nature of their duties resulted in the formation of a separate organisation. Now the W.A.A.F. is an integral part of the Royal Air Force. At the outbreak of the war there were five trades in which women could enrol. Now there are over sixty! The attractive uniform is air force blue, and badges of rank are identical with those of the R.A.F. showing close association with the fighting service.

stations. Being in charge, I wasn't always on the board. I might be sitting behind watching. All of a sudden, the Ops officer would ring down, and he'd ask for me. The girls would say, "For you, Corp." He'd say to me, "Air raid warning red." Once they'd heard me repeat Air raid warning, they used to take off their head sets and get out of my way!

I used to sit down quick, and plug up all the calls by heart, ring them all together, to save time, shove them all forward and call out, "Air raid warning red." That signal would go out to fire stations, police stations, and whoever had a siren. I had to wait for a few seconds, to make sure they'd all answered me, then I'd call out, "RAF Biggin Hill air raid warning red." That was if there was an immediate raid, where they'd come sneaking in without being spotted. Normally it was "air raid warning yellow." Afterwards you'd give the green warning, which meant they could sound the all-clear.

We used to do twelve hour shifts, from 8pm to 8am. Most of the time I was on night after night for more than twelve hours, because we were short of girls. There was no special training; you just picked it up as you went along. At Biggin Hill there must have been a couple of hundred extensions, and if there was a raid on and something had been hit, you had to know immediately where to plug in to tell the officer concerned, or to send the ambulance out onto the field. Sometimes I went for two or three days without going to sleep, because we'd been on all night. It got so bad one night at Biggin Hill, that the men wouldn't go on the top of the tower to do the fire watching. Only the WAAFs went on: the men were too scared to go up. The Ops officer came down with a tray of chewing gum and cigarettes. The place was shaking; it was terrible, so he said, "Have a cigarette," and that's what started me. I've never left off smoking since.

ADA (SMITHY) M/T

Joan Welch

I volunteered to go into the services. I didn't have to go, as I was working in the food industry in the Co-op. I could have been reserved, but I volunteered. A typical day in my life then, when I worked in the City, was picking our way to work through the debris, and finding the windows had come in on the machines. We somehow managed to do a day's work in spite of that. It seems funny, but I suppose being young it didn't worry me. We treated it as a bit of fun, picking our way through obstacles, and buildings actually falling where they'd been hit. I think the soldiers who came home on leave were more scared of being in London. They said "How can you women stand it?"

My brother had already been called up to go in the RAF, and I was a bit jealous really. I wasn't very happy at home, because my father had such a strict regime, and I thought I'd rather go. I was always a bit shy and reserved at home, and I thought it would probably be better to go into the services. The service pay wasn't a lot, but for a lot of people the firm would make their wages up to whatever they had been earning. As I volunteered, the Co-op didn't make my wages up. I just got the basic service pay. I can't remember how much it was, but it wasn't an awful lot. I was always hard up.

I started out at Innsworth, where you did basic training. I was there for about six weeks, and then they posted me up to Morecambe, to do actual training there, for another six weeks. Then I was posted back to Gloucester for training at the airfield there. I stayed there until they closed it down, and I got posted up to Reading, which was the head quarters for flying

training. I had a chance to go abroad, to Algiers, but I didn't like the idea, so I stayed.

At Staverton we had all the different courses coming in at the Air Observers school, and there was another training school over the road, Innsworth, so we had all sorts of poeple, Canadians and Americans. It was very nice. You found your friends, and birds of a feather stick together. There are people you don't get on with, but you find your own level. I was doing clerical work, general duties. It was mostly technical work really, filling in servicing forms for aircraft. They were on training flights, and they used to bring the forms in, so I'd get them up to date with the number of hours they'd flown, so they knew exactly how they were for maintenance.

When I was at Staverton there used to be some civilian families who would offer for you to go along to their homes for the evening to give you a break.

I got friendly with a nice family, a very well-to-do family at Churchdown, a little village nearby. We used to pick up a few rations in the cook house to take along there, because you wouldn't take anything of theirs. We used to cycle up there to see them in the village. It made a break. It was really quiet there as regards air raids, and as I was so worried about my family, I thought perhaps Mum and Dad would like to come down to Gloucester. I thought I'd go round the village and see if I could get accommodation for them to come down for a couple of weeks, to give them a break, but I couldn't find anywhere. It was full up because everyone was trying to get out of London. Eventually, the people who I used to go to for my evenings offered to put them up, so they kindly had them there, and they had a lovely couple of weeks. It gave them a break, because dad was getting into an awful state of nerves, what with what was going on in London.

The contraception then was the word "no". We couldn't go out with Canadians: they were too fast. We used to be cycling back, and the Americans used to pass in their jeep and try and hit you on the back and shout after you, but the Canadians wouldn't take "no", so we didn't go out with them.

JOAN OF ARCHIVES

Who keeps the A.P's up to date?
And decides for A.L's their ultimate fate?
Who, unwearying, with Amendments strives?
There's only one - Joan of Archives!

And now, Joan, you have "Come of Age"
And completed of your Life, one Page,
We hope you'll accept from Maintenance Wing,
The Good Wishes that this card will bring.

Three score and ten is a normal span
Two score and nine are left to plan.
We hope the lot will be filled with Joy,
And - if they're shared - by a very nice boy.

The Army, The Navy and The Air Force,
Have all appeared at times of course,
But if there isn't one you like
You need not go out and fall off your bike!

There's possibly one in Civilian Life,
Who thinks you'll make a very nice Wife,
His choice we're sure we all admire,
And we're also sure - He'll never tire!

-----oOo-----

Corporal Collins, the woman in charge, composed this poem. I used to work in a section called archives, and it's called "Joan of Archives". She composed it and then designed the card, and gave it to me on my twenty-first birthday. A friend of mine who also worked there lived at Worcester, which wasn't very far away. We had the same birthday, so I shared her twenty-first birthday party, at home where she lived.

ROYAL AIR FORCE
CERTIFICATE OF SERVICE AND RELEASE

of *Joan Elsie Lilian* SHEPHERD

The above-named airwoman served in the W.A.A.F. on full-time service,

from 30.10.42. to 24.6.46.

(*Last day of service in unit before leaving for release and release leave*).

Particulars of her Service are shown in the margin of this Certificate.

Brief statement of any special aptitudes or qualities or any special types of employment for which recommended :—

A very efficient Clerk. and possesses a retentive memory which has been of invaluable assistance to all concerned.

(T.W. INGHAM)
CAMP COMMANDANT
Signature of Officer Commanding

The worst thing that happened when I was in the services was having our leave stopped round about D Day. At the time we had to have innoculations done before we could go on leave. We got called up to have the innoculations done, and the next day they said all leave was cancelled. I was furious, what with a bad arm. We knew something was happening, because when we took a cycle ride, all the tanks and all the transport were all running through the country lanes in camouflage. The gliders used to go over from the Stoke Orchard airfield near us. There was a terrific load of activity going on around that time, and although it was all secret we knew something was going on.

For VE day I was at Reading. We went up to London, to Trafalgar Sqaure. We were all singing and dancing there. We had a job to get out of it, it was so packed. We were climbing over cars. It was just about a year after that, in 1946, that I came out of the services. You had to wait for your group to come up, to be demobbed. I had my job to go back to in the Co-op. I missed the company, but in some ways I was glad to get home. Hanging around waiting to be demobbed, we got a bit fed up with it. Going to live at home again was pretty grim, because Dad was always very strict. I was like having your wings clipped. I spent a lot of time round at a girl friend's.

I was assistant secretary, back at the Co-op. We just carried on as usual. I was lucky they kept my job open, because I had volunteered to go into the services. If I'd left it later I think they might not have. I went back there as though I had been called up. My service continued in the Co-op.

Patricia

I was still at school at the start of the war. Father was a Territorial, so he was called up immediately. I had one brother. My mother put down to be a helper with the evacuees, so we went down from Greenwich to Southborough, near Tunbridge Wells. The family who took us in had an oast house. They used the base as garages, and people lived over the garage. They had six camp beds up for six boys. They put a couple of beds up in the circular part of the oast house, and my mother and I had those. In those days you didn't think they were crowded: it was a way of life.

We went in '39, and I was quickly bored. I went back to London and left mother with the boys, and went to live with my grandparents. Then, in '40, the blitz came, the bombing of London. My grandparents wouldn't move while I was in the house, so eventually I saw sense and moved back to Southborough. I got a couple of jobs and finished up with the Inland Revenue in Tunbridge Wells. I joined up with two other girls who, like myself, thought we could do something better and volunteered. One changed her mind, one went in the army, and I decided on the blue. There was something about the air force boys. I married a soldier, but there you are.

I was down in Southborough, but I think it was Tonbridge where I actually reported and had my medicals and got my call up. I had hammer toes and they weren't sure whether they wanted me with hammer toes. I had no problems walking, and I managed my square-bashing alright. I did that in Gloucester. It was part of the passing out. I suppose you realise there's got to be discipline, you've got to do these things and there are better things to come. It was just something you had to do. You can't rebel the minute you've volunteered for something, can you?

It was all women in charge. You were always responsible to one, and when you were posted away you'd always got your WAAF officer in charge of you.

" *We're reporting to you to start the unarmed combat course!* "

We lived in a typical old nissan hut, with a big fire in the centre. It was warm when the fire was on, and the nearer the fire you were, the warmer you were. You had to learn to live in a small space with all sorts and kinds. You couldn't pick your billet. When you're under one roof you get on with it as best you can. Although we didn't have much room at home, we were brought up with a little bit of privacy. You could do your own thing. There was no privacy in a nissan hut.

I went into Special Duties initially. That was my fancy. When the boys were flying off we had to be up at the station, and there they were dished out with their bits and pieces. I took to riding a bicycle to get from our quarters to the station. The pilots were briefed there and got their information. At least we were in on a certain amount of highly secret information. We knew roughly where they were going, and we saw how many were going, and of course we were always watching and waiting for them to come back, hoping they'd all make it.

Unfortunately, that didn't last long, because I didn't manage to get my LACW, Leading Air Craft Woman. You go in as ACW2, Air Craft Woman 2, and you become an ACW I, First Class, and then you get your wings, as they called them, for Leading Air Craft Woman. Operations Intelligence was what I was hoping to do.'' Clerk Special Duties,'' as they called it. It wasn't clerical work as we know clerical work today. It was all secrets as to where the boys were flying to. Presumably there were too many of us wanting to do that sort of work, because they decided, soon after I got there, that we had to remuster. As I say, I hadn't got my Leading Air Craft Woman, and after that there was nothing but cooking and waitressing, or being an orderly, that sort of work. Apart from that there was wages and pay clerks, so they sent me to Penarth, and I did a course down there, learning how to do pay accounts. Then they sent me from there to a place called Gravely. That was a new station. It wasn't operational, so you felt out of touch with things. Well, I did. When you're on an operational station you get much more into what's going on and how the war's going.

When it was pay day for the forces, you had a male officer with you, and I was the one who called the names. Whoever it was would come up and salute, and give their last three numbers. If I couldn't get my figures to balance, then it was hard work, but that was just me, because I hadn't got the knack. There's got to be people doing the mundane tasks, but it wasn't for me, pay accounts, really.

I'd already met my husband before I got myself called up into the RAF, and I got married on my first leave. We got married in uniform. My spare time occupation was anything going on in the station. They put films and that sort of thing on, and we did write letters to each other, and that took up time as well. When I was in the WAAF, I didn't have any contact with the American service men, but Tunbridge Wells was full of them. They'd got the money, they'd got the know-how. There was something very different about them from our boys. Some were charming, some were not so nice. They seemed to have access to the nylons, which were precious. Anything for a nice pair of sheers!

I never had any thoughts of being an officer. I was only an ACW2, the lowest of the low. As I went in, so I came out. They gave me three months sick leave when they discovered I was pregnant. I had a super discharge report, saying that everything was excellent, and then at the bottom they spoilt it, because I was not recommended for going back in. Obviously they'd decided that I wasn't a good bet. It was nothing to do with my character, but I wasn't recommended to go further. I suppose I'd rather wasted their time, what with the training and the kitting out. I was so taken up with the baby, though, I had other things to think about. I'd gone back to basics. I just wanted to be a mum. I wanted four children, and I even overstepped the mark there: I had five. I had no great ambitions, I don't think. The urge for children was greater. It wasn't until I went back to work, when my youngest son was 12, that I suddenly thought maybe I'd been a bit stupid and I could have had a career.

Bill Welch

At the tail end of the war I'd done two years in the Mediterranean, then I came home and worked on the submarines. Then they found out that when I first went in the navy I'd had pneumonia, so I was unfit for submarine service. They gave me a shore job up in Glasgow, on the merchant ships that used to carry soap and oil. Some of them carried guns, and those guns were maintained by the navy and the army on board ship. They called them the DEMS, the Defence of Merchant Shipping, and I was attached to them. These merchant ships used also to carry mine-sweeping apparatus called paravanes, and they would be serviced every time the ship came into port.

I was in change of six "Jenny Wrens", and we used to go round these merchant ships to service those paravanes. Directly the chaps on board saw these girls,

they'd say, "What would you like? You can have anything you want." The girls'd get on board and say, "Where's the officers mess then?" We'd get down there, have tea, and get the eggs and bacon going. On merchant ships they used to have plenty of grub going, so we used to do alright.

We were allowed our tea breaks and our dinner breaks, and then we used to find out where the paravanes were, and the equipment that goes with them to be serviced, and we'd spend about three days on one ship, doing these. We used to take our time, if it was a nice ship, and a nice mess. The WRNS loved playing crib: the old green board'd come out with the cards, and they'd be playing all day.

We were billetted in the WRNS quarters in Glasgow, just off Sauchiehall Street. We had a little place there, and it was lovely. I enjoyed going there.

A damsel high up in the WAAF, said: "I'm grateful to Wolsey not HAAF! With their undies and hose, and their frocks a girl knows she can always keep on the right PAAF!"

Wolsey

Whatever you buy now must wear as never before. Remember Wolsey gives you the best value for your coupons

Uniforms and Equipment.

Maria Tardios

I came to England from Cyprus before the war. My brother was already here, so I wrote to him and he had an invitation made out to me to come to England. When I came, I came to work and stay.

During the war I was making government surplus clothing, trousers and jackets. I was put on sewing pads for the soldiers' cuffs, which would change colour, if the Germans dropped the gas.

I sewed a brown piece of paper like material, triangular in shape, covered in a solution, which melted the pads of your fingers, on to these cuffs. They used to have buckets of liquid, so we could soak our fingers to try and heal them. We would make one hundred pieces for 2/-. We used to earn £1/10/- a week.

Dolores.

I was born in North Africa, in Tangiers. My father-in-law and my husband were British, so that's how I came over to Britain. We left Tangiers in December, 1941, on a beautiful Polish liner. There was our boat, and two destroyers, and we sailed out in convoy. The journey only took four days. We arrived in Greenock, and the WVS were waiting for us with lovely hot soup and warm clothes for anyone who wanted them. We came off the boat and went straight onto the train, and went right down to London.

We were living in the National Hotel, where people like us were billetted. I was so far away from home, and I missed my family. I was crying and crying. My husband didn't want me to go to work, but I begged him to let me go with another girl who was living in the hotel. We went to work at a Kings Cross beer factory. I was quite happy, putting labels on the bottles, and then I was put on a machine in the basement. I left, because it was making me feel so dizzy. Then I went to work for a Gibraltarian person, in a very small firm in Soho. We used to put the ribbon round the Australian army hats, the hats with curled up brims. After we put the ribbon on, we put a hook to curl it up.

At the beginning, living in England was very hard. We weren't allowed any rations books at first, so we were supplied by the Lyons Company and, of course, the food wasn't very good. I used to go out on the black market and bring home food, rice, a bit of cooking fat. Sometimes I would come home crying when I could not get what I wanted because they would not give it to me.

There was a small shop in Marchmont Street, where you could go to get black market goods. Sometimes you had to wait, if there were customers in the shop. We had to be very careful, because we were putting them in an awkward position. You could get everything there; sugar and rice, and rib of bacon. We used to buy all the bones and make a beautiful pea soup. After the war was finished, if they saw me coming, they'd say, "Do you want the bones?" and I'd say, "Not now. I want the bacon!"

Mrs. Pitt

In the First World War I did gas masks. I worked at Spicers near Southwark Bridge, in Union Street. We used to paint round the holes made by stitching in gas masks, to make sure the gas couldn't get in. Also we used to put sticky plaster on card. There were two holes on the card and we used to put string through them and tie it together. That went with the gas mask, so when the gas masks were given out, they were given the card as well. If the gas got through the stitching holes, the soldiers used to peel off the plaster from the card and put it in the hole. I used to take them home for my mum to work on as well.

Jean Batcham

Before my husband went abroad he was stationed in Exeter. The local people were asked to entertain the troops for Christmas in their homes, so my husband and another fellow were entertained by some people, and they invited me down for a fortnight. I had to do war work there, night work, the navy blue silk parachutes for the RAF. You used a copper needle with thick white cotton, and an examiner would get either end and pull them. If there were any stitches to crack, they would make them crack. They couldn't take any chances at all, because if they cracked when they were bailing out or anything it would have been so dangerous. They pulled and pulled, and probably you sat there all night working and you had to go all over it again.

We used to have the ENSA show at midnight. It was good entertainment, fellas and girls all dressed up in the RAF, army and naval uniforms. They'd come marching on and sing all the latest songs, and we'd all join in. We'd have one hour, and then all go back to our machines. We'd have to work till 8 o'clock in the morning. I got the sack from there because I took too much time off. When my husband was on leave I used to take time off and go back home. Very often I would get a letter or a telegram saying, ''Come immediately: home bombed''. It used to happen quite a lot, but one day, when I came back, the Governor said, ''Here's your cards. You've got the sack.'' I stayed in Exeter so long because my mum would write and say that the raids were terrible, and to try and stay down there. I remember that one night my husband came in and said he was going abroad. After upsetting myself and everybody else, it turned out he was only going to the docks at Cardiff in Tiger Bay. He was stuck there for a long time. After that he was sent off to Gibraltar, and he stayed there all during the war. I was pregnant, so I went home to my mother.

I was always doing stitching work during the war. I went to another place, in the Old Kent Road, to make ARP overalls. It was a firm that made marquees for all the big weddings. I made covers for the wheels of aeroplanes as well. They were made out of stuff like leather. I had one gruesome job, making body bags, long body bags for the dead, and little bags to attach to them for the jewellery. They used to be sent back saturated in blood, and that had to be ripped out and a new piece sewn in. Nothing was ever wasted.

WAR WORK TRUE STORIES, NO. 5

From designing gowns... to making guns!

1. Seriously injured when bombed-out, Mrs. Burton considered what she could do to "get her own back on Hitler!"

2. After a speech by Mr. Bevin she decided temporarily to give up designing dresses and go into War Work!

3. In a Government Training Centre she was taught a new job and made swift progress in her training.

4. Now a seasoned worker in a war factory, Mrs. Burton is doing a grand, worth-while job for her country.

You can also help—Go TO-DAY to your Local Office of the Ministry of Labour and National Service, and they will tell you how you can best serve your country.

Your duty now is WAR WORK

These stories are founded on fact, but the names used are fictitious.

ISSUED BY THE MINISTRY OF LABOUR AND NATIONAL SERVICE

HOW TO SPEND LESS ON SHOES - even with prices so high

She put her foot in her letters until . .

You must make shoes last longer now. It's a national duty. Leather is scarce and shoes will cost more and more. Every time you buy new shoes or have old ones repaired get Phillips Stick-a-Soles and

Phillips Heels fitted. Phillips Soles are fixed firm as a rock with Phillips solution only—if your shoes just need heeling, fit Phillips Heels. Phillips save you money at every step.

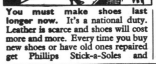

Phillips STICK-A-SOLES and PHILLIPS HEELS

Phillips Soles and Heels are entirely British made.

Mrs Burtenshaw

I served an apprenticeship in dressmaking just before the war. I was getting 6/- a week. We used to do two garments a week, and they were 50 guineas each. I worked there for nine years until I got married. Once you got married they didn't like you to go back to work. I was home for about three years. I had a daughter, and we were bombed out, so we had no home, no nothing. That's when I went on war work at Hamptons, in Queen's Road, Battersea.

Being a dress-maker, it was a bit humiliating, but I needed the money. I went down there to see if they needed anyone, and they did. It was a very happy place. It was piece work. We started on chin straps for the soldiers, and we used to get one shilling for twelve of them. We had khaki with great big buckles, and we had to stitch in between. We went on to khaki belts and Russian sleeping bags. They were vast, and as white as snow. We had to stuff them with kapok, and stitch them in sections, so the kapok would stay in. We did handkerchiefs for the Americans as well. They were a ha' penny each. The border had to be half an inch all the way round, and they folded them corner-wise to make sure the were square. Terribly precise, the Americans. Americans.

When we'd run out of things to do, we had to go home. I was glad, because I could work very quickly, earn my money by dinner time and go home. I used to go in at 8 o'clock until 1 o'clock. If we got more work I would stay till about 3 or 4, five days a week. It was nearly all women. Some of the women working with me had children, but they had been evacuated, so that's why the women could work. There were creches: I can think of one I knew in Clapham, Larkhall Rise. I think it may have been private. There was nothing attached to our factory. When things got bad, they did ask us if we wanted to take our children and go to Barnstable, because they had another factory in Barnstable where they would have looked after the children. When the raids got bad, I used

to take my daughter to work with me. Sometimes we had to work on Sunday if there was a rush of work on, and I'd take her then. I found I'd do a little bit of work and then run off to the shelter. Hamptons had a shelter below ground. You'd run to the shelter, and be worried all the time you were down there, because you were losing money.

The room we worked in was full of heavy machines. No carpets, nothing like that. It was bare broads and no comforts. The sewing machines were on benches in rows and rows, and we had chairs that swivelled round. The sewing machine that I was on was very large, with a big wheel and a big foot pedal. The needle was about three and a half inches. I saw girls get the needle in their thumbs. That was dreadful, and there was no compensation. We threaded the machines ourselves. It was thick thread. You had to be careful not to get your material caught in the wheel of the machine, because you could stop the power of the machines and stop everybody's work. If your machine went wrong you had to book the mechanic. Joe the mechanic was a Jew, and very nice. He did the work of about half a dozen. In the middle of the room there were work boxes, and you'd have to put the finished work in there. There was a woman who counted it to make sure you'd put your dozen in. Then we'd go to a table to the forelady, and she'd give us the other work that we needed.

We were arranged in rows, so we could talk, but you had to keep your eye on that needle. We had "Music While You Work," and you would sit at your machine to have your cup of tea. Perhaps your neighbour might bring it to you. You'd get one another's to save time. Sometimes you would sit there and eat your sandwiches. You could have a lunch break, but that was in your own time. We provided our own overalls; we weren't supplied with anything. You didn't have to tie your hair up, just be careful it didn't get caught in the machines.

Mrs. Dubus

When the war started I was working in what was called direct mail advertising, at Wallaces in High Holborn, but after six months all that advertising was stopped, so we lost our jobs. You either had to do war work, or go in the services, if you weren't married. I met a friend who was out of work, and she said, "Will you come with me to the Labour Exchange? They're going to send me for a job." So we went and signed on. They used to give you a green ticket to take to the firm you were sent to. I went with her to Schweppes Kiaora, as it was called in those days, and the manager said to me,

"Aren't you working?"

"No," I said. "I've just got put off."

He said, "Would you like to come and work here?"

I said I had never done that sort of work, but he said it was easy and I'd get used to it. So, I did it. It's better than being out of work.

I'd been there two months, and this man came in one day, who I knew. He was the manager of some other place I'd worked in, and he was now working here. I was called into the office by this manager one day, and he said, "You know Maggie is leaving to have a baby. Would you like to do her labelling job."

I said, "I've only just come in. You should offer that to someone who has been here a while."

"But I know you can do it," he said, "Some of them just want a job where you don't use much skill. I know you can do numbering."

Whoever did the job of labelling the bottles had a little room to herself. The labels were all different shapes, little neck labels and square labels, shiny or not. There was a paper shortage, but they got their labels alright. You had to put a number on the label when it was made, so that if there was a complaint about the contents of the bottle, they knew what vat it had come from. The label showed the date and what vat number it was. In the morning the manager would come in and say "We're going to do 3,000 bitter lemon." You'd get those labels out and put the date on them with your date stamp, and then they'd go upstairs to the girls on the labelling machines. Next they would go to other girls who would wrap cellophane round them and screw the tops on, to make them look all nice. If the bottles were going abroad they went in wooden boxes. They were exported to the troops.

We used to do stock taking over two days, but I always knew exactly what I had in my boxes because I used to write what I had on my cards. Each time I took 3,000 labels out, I just took 3,000 off the list, so I didn't have to count, because I knew exactly what was in there. The

manager used say, "You've done that stock taking perfect." It only took an hour, but I never told him that.

The factory was noisy because of the bottling machines. But the girls used to sing, because they didn't have to keep their mind on that sort of work. We had an Irish lady and there's not a voice as good on the telly

Large Midland factory has vacancies for night-shift work, alternating with day-shift. Railway fares and expenses paid for interview.

WOMEN! IF YOU ARE 31 OR OVER

and not engaged on essential work, please write today stating your age, and whether married or single, to

Box 716, G.L.G.P., 92 Fleet Street, E.C.4

A spirit of determination is sweeping through Britain today. It is alive in the women who are taking up night shift work in our great factories — the spirit which today and tonight is driving our machines full speed ahead to victory.

ENROL TODAY SPECIAL PAY AND PRIVILEGES

today. She used to sing nearly all day. One day was St Patrick's day and she said to the girls, "Let's have a sing song this afternoon with all the Irish songs". She used to sing all the Irish songs and my favourite one, "I may not be an Angel". The Manager said to her one day, "Mary, I don't mind you singing, but please lower your voice. I'm sure they can hear you in Blackfriars Road."

I started at 8 in the morning and finished at 5 at night. You had $^3/_4$ hour for your break. We didn't have a canteen, so those who lived near enough used to pop home. The rest of us used to bring some rolls and get a cup of tea. You had a cup of tea during the morning, and we would have lunch together.

There wasn't a union, but it was a good job. We got about £2 a week. There were men to do the heavy work, and they got about £2/10/-. You didn't get overtime. I was happy when they said this was a reserved occupation, because it was an easy job.

SALVAGE YOUR WASTE PAPER

It is more than ever necessary that every piece of waste paper should go to help the war effort. Make it your personal duty to collect every scrap you can.

Administration.

Beverley

During the First World War, I had an interview at the Labour Exchange, and when I told them I could write and add up and everything, they sent me to the records offices at Woolwich Dockyard. I worked there for about 3 years.

Letters would come from wives about their husbands and I'd write it in their records. We didn't answer the letters, some other office did. I learnt a lot about soldiers. Some would be carrying on with someone else and the wives would write a letter about it. I had to write that down on his sheet. That would go to the Head Office and they'd enquire about it. Any enquiry that came in about a soldier I would put on this sheet. The information would be sent to that man's officer, no matter what part of Europe it was. I only dealt with living soldiers. Some might have stopped their wives allowance and they'd enquire about it. They'd carry on with some other woman and stop the allowance. I don't know how they did it. The wife would want to know why her allowance was stopped and I'd write it down and have nothing more to do with it. It was interesting work.

The 1st World War was shocking. I thought there'd never be another war, and then it came along. I was married then, and I had three children. I had to have them evacuated, and they went to Devon. I stayed in London, because my husband was sick in Lewisham Hospital, from being gassed in the First World War. I went to the Borough and passed the exam for a postwoman. I was a postwoman at Greenwich Park. I was sent to Park Street, and I had to be up there early in the blackout. That's what ruined my eyes, coming out of the blackout into a bright light, sorting the letters. At that time there were 3 deliveries a day, and a lot of the young women used to be waiting for their army letters at 9.30am. You'd deliver at 8 o'clock, go back, sort some more letters out at the office, and deliver in the afternoon. Then you'd do the 5.30 delivery. You'd be at home for two or three hours in between to do your house work or shopping. We paid money into a union. I always joined. I was never against anything like that. It paid you to, really. There were still men working in the sorting office. They were too old to go into the army. I never found out if they were paid the same.

I got fed up with walking round with the post, so I went to the Prudential office in Nelson Street and got a job there. I collected insurance money and paid out sick benefit. I took over the round of a chap who had gone overseas. Some of them were very hard to get the money out of because they'd spend it on beer. You'd meet all types. One flat you'd go into would be spotless, then you'd go next door, and, oh boy, you'd learn a lot. If the siren went while I was collecting I would either go to the shelter, or if I was in somebody's house, they'd say, "Stay here for a little while." It didn't matter staying with strangers. Really we were rather jocular.

When the Second World War was declared I felt disappointed that we had to face another lot. I think the women in the war were wonderful. When I was a postwoman, I didn't like doing the late delivery at all, in the blackout, but you had to face it. You couldn't hum and ha about it, you had to get on with your job. Women

SALESGIRL BY DAY **CANTEEN WORKER BY NIGHT**

YOUR EYES ARE DOING Double Time

Voluntary duties at night, following a full day's work, often in the glare of artificial light, impose a severe strain on the eyes. To safeguard your sight, you should have your eyes examined at least every two years. Go to a Qualified Optician on the H.S.A. Official List for expert advice and moderate charges.

H.S.A. OPTICIANS ARE CARRYING ON!

Look for the Shield Sign   *in the Window!*

CONSULT A QUALIFIED OPTICIAN ON THE H.S.A. OFFICIAL LIST

took on any job. Women do, don't they? They've got more guts than men! Men don't know half of it, really.

Rose Mullett

I was in London all through the war, in the middle of London, all around Grosvenor Square. I had a bedsit and I paid £3 guineas a week. That was a lot, but I could afford it at the time, because my husband was in the army and I had his allowance and I was earning £6 a week working for the Americans.

When the war first started, I was working for a firm of civil engineers in Park Lane, and they owned the Dorchester. They had built it and they thought it would be safer for them to move into it, which they did. The particular department I was in occupied the ball room. No public functions were allowed then in the war, so all our things were set up on this great pile carpet in the ball room.

We used to trot to and fro across this floor, which was almost like a trampoline, to get to our work, and they left the chandeliers so we worked by the light of them. I did this for some time.

I then had to go for an interview with the Ministry of Labour. They decided that work wasn't important enough, so I was directed to work for the Americans.

My first job with them, ironically enough, was in a hotel, the Cumberland at Marble Arch, equally luxurious. Later they moved into the annexe of Selfridge's which was shut. It was horrible in there, because everything was boarded up and the whole thing had been partitioned. The smell of this wood when you went in!

When I was working in the Selfridge annexe, there was a Lyons ordinary tea shop, not a corner house, across the road, and the British gave the Americans this Lyons for their canteen. We were able to use it for our lunch times and we had all this luscious food. This went on and then it got demolished by a bomb and we didn't get another one.

We did have lots of perks really. I suppose you'd call them perks. We were able to buy things from what they called their PX's a sort of canteen. We could buy things like cigarettes and chocolates and nylons.

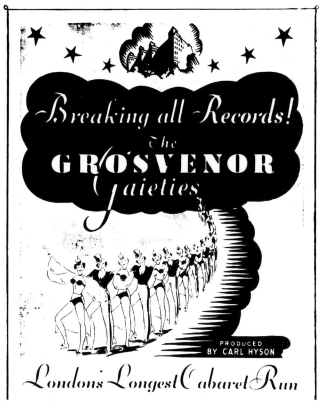

Breaking all Records!
The GROSVENOR Gaieties
PRODUCED BY CARL HYSON
London's Longest Cabaret Run

The work was rather dreary. I was in charge of some offices and what they called procurement. That meant obtaining all their office supplies, and newspapers for the forces all over Britain. I used to go all round London trying to locate the books for the Americans, like Jane's Fighting Ships. Some of them were hard to get. I also obtained typewriters and stationery for them.

I think some of the Americans thought the Civil War was still on, because they absolutely loathed the Northerners. My boss was from Virginia and he'd say: "Get those damn Yankees out of here," if they came into his office.

I don't know how we got any work done, because they kept moving. We were always packing and moving next door. It all worked very well though.

When the Americans had just arrived, when the doodlebugs came round, they were terrified. They'd say: "What do we do? What do we do?" Of course, we were calm, because we were used to it. The Americans would insist on going down to the shelters all the time, but then they got used to it.

We knew when it was coming up to D-Day, because of the great activity going on. When you're working in that sort of thing yourself, you don't understand it, it's all secret, but it was important war work really.

At the end of the war I stayed on to compile the American roll of honour, of servicemen who died over here. I could have stayed there and worked for the Embassy, but I was expecting a child by then so I gave up.

I was quite a theatre-goer during the war. With me working there, I could go along at lunch time or in the evening and get a ticket. If a raid occurred, they used to announce it, so you could go out if you wished. The performance would still carry on. At first people tended to go out, but later they didn't. "The Windmill" used to say: "We never close." A lot of stars made their names there. Once I had seen everything in London that I wanted to, really wanted to. Now I can't afford it.

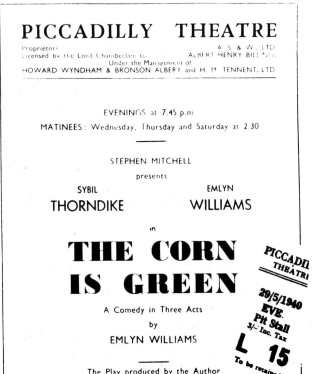

PICCADILLY THEATRE

Proprietors A S & W, LTD
Licensed by the Lord Chamberlain to ALBERT HENRY BILLING
Under the Management of
HOWARD WYNDHAM & BRONSON ALBERY and H. M. TENNENT, LTD

EVENINGS at 7.45 p.m
MATINEES: Wednesday, Thursday and Saturday at 2.30

STEPHEN MITCHELL
presents

SYBIL   EMLYN
THORNDIKE   WILLIAMS

in

THE CORN IS GREEN

A Comedy in Three Acts
by
EMLYN WILLIAMS

The Play produced by the Author

PICCADILLY THEATRE
29/5/1940
EVE.
Pit Stall
3/- Inc. Tax
L 15
To be retained

Joy Brown

At the very beginning of the war, I was in Taunton Somerset. A sleepy Somerset town, surrounded by hills, damp all the year round. It may be a lovely area for exploring, but when there's no transport, as there was in the war, it wasn't much fun. I was there in 1939, and my immediate reaction was — the forces for me! I thought I'll get out of this old bank and do something a little bit more interesting.

So I went down to the offices to join the forces and I was told: "No, you're in a reserved occupation." And this went on right through the war. I went so many times to try and get into the forces, and I didn't care if it was the WAAFS, ATS, or the WRENS. My friends had all got in, but not me.

What they did do was to take women between 20 to 21, who were born between certain months, from all the banks in the country. They had to go whether they wanted to or not. But not me! They didn't take anymore after that, because they reckoned we were doing a man's job.

I got a bit fed up with sleepy Somerest, so I used the excuse of my parents having gone to Yorkshire, and that they weren't well, to get a transfer. So I went to the Leeds branch right in the centre of town. It was a busy branch. It certainly wasn't sleepy! I always stick up for Leeds. I thought it was a marvellous place, and there was such an atmosphere of bustle, and the Yorshire people were so friendly. It was quite different from being in Somerset.

I went to the Leeds branch as a secretary, which is what I was. Gradually they put us on the jobs that the men were doing, and I ended up on this very busy counter at Leeds, at the age of 23.

In those days no men went on the counter at 23. They had to be at least 30, and before they were appointed a cashier, and no girl ever was!

My salary remained on the exact same scale as it was if I'd been doing machine work. I used to get £10 a year extra, because I had shorthand and typing qualifications, although I wasn't using them. So I was on the counter, working for 28/- a week to start with, and after that it rose by about 5/- a year. It never went up by anymore than if I'd been doing ordinary tapping out on the machine or adding up. The bank never paid the ladies anymore for doing men's work.

I remember the Bank Officers Guild people coming in to try to get us to sign on the dotted line to join the Bank Officers Guild.

We all joined, but not a thing came of it. We felt we were being a bit hard done by. I mean, I worked all the hours of the night, I really did. At the end of a day's work, when you'd done all the counter work, you counted up and then had to go back and do the machine work. Night after night, I didn't get home till eight o'clock. If it was fifteen shillings out you stayed there to find it. If that happened you'd get home at 11pm. There was no overtime pay for this at all.

Although it wasn't war work, as such, it was jolly hard work.

I tried to volunteer for the Home Guard, because in Leeds there wasn't very much you could do if you weren't skilled. So I went to the Home Guard, quite a few of us did, and I did the training.

There was a special women's section and we'd be on duty in factories and things like that. I was sent to guard a clothing factory. It sounds odd guarding a clothing factory, but there you are. Unfortunately my hours in the bank were so erratic, that I had to give it up. Every time I put my name down for doing duties, I couldn't get away, so it fizzled out. In a way the bank was my life.

When all the men came back after the war, the bank said: "Thank you very much for doing all the work for our men while they've been away, but we're not going to have ladies on the counter. Now you've got to teach the men."

I had a lieutenant commander for about a fortnight. He was really as dim as you could make him, when it came to totting up money and all the rest of it. He'd say: "Joy, I'm never going to do it." I said: "I'm sorry, you've just got to learn, Brian, you've got to do it." After that a lieutenant colonel had to learn. He was a bit quicker on the uptake. They took over on the counter and we watched them for a week and stood by them for a week and watched them do the work, and then we went back to the jolly old machines, the ledger machines, and the statement machines, and the shorthand and typing. They did all the work.

The bank increased the number on the counter, because by this time a lot of the staff were coming back, so, of course, they could do. Instead of having four of us working on this whole large counter in Leeds, they had seven men, most of whom had come from the war. They'd been away, some of them had gone away in 1940, and they came back in 1946/7, so they were seven years older, so they had to get trained for the cashier's job. They'd finished their mundane jobs at the back doing the ledgers, so they must start up the scale.

We didn't get paid extra for teaching the men. We still stayed on the same scale we had come in on. You started on a scale at about eighteen-years old and you'd reach the top by about age thirty-three. After that you'd have your rises and increments according to the whims of the management. There were no special perks for doing special jobs.

In those days we had to wear navy blue alpaca overalls, and I can tell you, they were horrible. They were stiff, they were shiny, alpaca was a shiny material. It was hard like shiny paper, and the overalls buttoned up and had a belt round that was always coming undone and didn't really do up properly. Underneath we couldn't wear anything very bright, it had to be subdued.

I read a bank magazine the other day and it started off: "Gone are the alpaca overalls, forever, we hope."

TYPEWRITERS

PORTABLE & STANDARD machines required for urgent Government work. Highest prices paid. Send us particulars.

All makes of guaranteed Typewriters for sale at moderate prices, write or telephone

FLEET TYPEWRITER CO.
117 Fleet Street, London, E.C.4

Telephone : CENTRAL 7162

Tess

When war broke out I was doing market research, and on the day they started evacuating the kids, I was checking up on the amount of display work in Woolworth's stores in the West End.

I remember, when we went back to the office, there was a notice on the door, saying that they'd evacuated themselves to the country and to send the material to them and they'd send us our money. They suggested we go to our local town hall and offer to do national registration work.

Well off I went to my town hall in Wandsworth and they started me right away! I had to collate all the information on the national registration forms. This same register was used to do ration books later.

I was working in this job about a year, when suddenly I was called up to the office to see the food officer. He told me that I was to go to the Ministry of Supply for an interview straight away.

I went in to see the bloke in charge. He looked at me and said: "Let me ask you something. If you were to address six hundred women with the idea of recruiting them into war work, what would you say?"

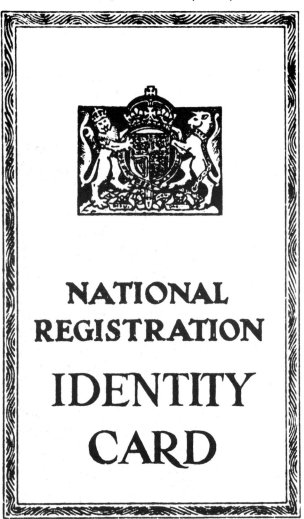

NATIONAL
REGISTRATION
IDENTITY
CARD

I said: "I shouldn't allow myself to get into such a ridiculous situation. I wouldn't attempt to get women to do war work unless I knew a good deal more about it than I do at the moment." "Oh" he looked. Anyway, I was engaged as a Labour Supply officer. I rang and asked my Mum to put a case together for me. It was collected in a taxi and I was up in Staffordshire the same

night in this filling factory. That's how you did things in the war. Things could be done speedily and decisions could be made. I came highly recommended, so that was it. I ended up in the factory that night.

Recruiting people was a combined operation. The Ministry of Supply would have a project; either its own ordnance factory had to be staffed, or a factory which was on their priority list for supplies. Where there were labour shortages there would be a conference at the Ministry of Supply on the labour position. Then somebody would be delegated the job of going into it to see what sources there were available in the locality. With this staffordshire filling factory, they wanted very large numbers of women and a lot of factories were closing down in Bradford. The Ministry of Information did publicity, Ministry of Labour set up labour bureaux, and women could come in off the street, and try out the machines they would work on. I set up what happened in the factory for guests and looked after the billetted girls.

We'd have a big parade in a town with a mock up tank say, and girls from a factory marching in their work clothes. This was all to get more recruits to join the factory, to create an atmosphere for them to want to join.

We'd hold meetings all over a town and hand out leaflets, and with part time workers, we'd have girls from the factories in the area going out in a van and talking about the jobs they did.

In the evening, we'd hold a concert in the town hall and any girl, who came into the bureaux during the day

WOMEN OF BRITAIN
COME INTO
THE FACTORIES
ASK AT ANY EMPLOYMENT EXCHANGE FOR ADVICE AND FULL DETAILS

would be given a free ticket and we'd have possibly Olivier doing Shakespeare, an orchestra and I remember Cyril Smith coming to one.

We did human interest stories on a gran, who was the best time keeper in her section, and you might have granny with a young airman who she was producing things for. This would be put into magazines.

Labour was gold, there was a tremendous shortage of labour, and we needed to increase production. Production was the word, not profit, or finance. You needed every pair of hands you could get, if you were serious about winning the war.

We set up joint production committees with the trade unions and the employers. That was to see we got effective production. Everything was subordinated to it.

I visited factories, who were on Ministry of Supply contracts, if they were having labour supply problems, if they were underproducing, or to see if they were carrying out the terms of their contract.

I remember one instance when we got a request to go into a factory in Birmingham, that produced dressings and sanitary towels, because they were having trouble getting labour. When I went down to see the young man in charge of the production side there he said: "You know it's terribly distressing, because when you're trying to get people to stay on the job or to come to a job, they can understand the wound dressings and bandages being part of the war work, but it's very difficult to make them understand that sanitary towels are a necessary part of things we have to provide for the women in the forces."

These young girls were being grabbed by everybody. They thought they were doing their bit, but when they got shoved on to sanitary towels they used to leave and do something that was nearer to the war work.

Towards the end of the war some private firms were doing some of the work in small filling factories, to get extra production and I sometimes discovered that these private firms were cutting corners on safety regulations. They'd say to me: "We're not as fussy they are," meaning the government factories, and I always said: "This has been worked out on the experience of the First World War and it is a condition of your contract. We cannot afford to have accidents, people suffering from yellow skin disease, or dermatitis."

There were agreements made between the government and the unions, concerning women working. There was an agreement about the dilution of labour, the return of men from the war, salary scales, that kind of thing. If a woman went into a job that had previously been done by a man, she got a good rate of pay. In terms of relative skill, women got paid the same as the men. It was on a skilled rate. In a number of cases the wage rate was fixed for the job, on the basis that when the men came back from the war and wanted their jobs, the women would leave them.

For many women the war became a liberating thing. It took them out from under the eyes of their neighbours

Women engaged in making parts for telephones

and all the conventions and social pressures they had been under. I thought it was tremendously important for them to find out what they could do. I knew, and had always felt, women could do most of the things that anybody else did.

WOMEN
please lend your support a little longer…

let's work together for

PROSPERITY

The women tackled things with such spirit. There was a marvellous woman in a foundry. She'd been in the Music Halls, and she was a welfare officer. She said "I've only got two qualifications for being a welfare officer, I've got a good bosom to cry on, and I can make a damn good cup of tea." She said that the big trouble with the women was that they'd chuck everything they'd got into it, to prove they could do it. "I stand by for the first three days, while they throw themselves into it, and I know on the third day I'm going to have showers of tears, and teaslined up, with plenty of hankies. They don't understand that to do a day's work you've got to pace it. It's no good putting everything you've got into the first hour. You've got to do a bit, stop, and that's why the jokes about the workman leaning on his shovel by a hole are so stupid. You can't work at full pelt for eight hours in a day." The women learned to do that and then they were fine. They needed sufficient training that's all.

I never believed that women couldn't do things because they weren't tough enough. Some women are tough and some men aren't tough. I didn't believe it was necessary at that time, as it isn't now, for people to lift heavy things about, or have to do physically heavy work. There are enough devices and equipment to make it unnecessary. It seemed to me a tremendous opportunity for women to find out what they could do. Not only in doing the work, but manageing their families and affairs and while the men were away.

I watched a whole lot of women bloom when they found that they could do all these things that they had been told they couldn't do, and they enjoyed the feeling that they could learn and put their hands to anything that turned up. I watched the older women find that they were necessary. We were all necessary and needed, the country couldn't get on without us.

For myself, my own confidence was boosted by tackling things that I'd never done before.

If somebody at the end of the war had said "Take over an industry", I wouldn't have done it without being frightened, but I would have had a go.

Eileen Smith

I went to work in Matchless Motorcycles in August 1936 and I was still working there, when war broke out. I tried to volunteer for the forces, but I failed the medica because of my heart. Well, six months later I had a letter from the Labour Exchange to say that I was going to be sent up to munitions in Scotland. Of course, they never gave any reason why Scotland, and there were local munitions factories I could have gone to. I was only 20 or 21, but the girl who interviewed me was younger than I was. She was over officious, and had to spend all her time working from papers in front of her. She was only following the rules I suppose. She said to me: "You've got to go" and I said: "There's no 'got to' about it." "Alright then," she said: "You'll go to prison." I said: "Alright then, send me to prison." She didn't say anything, and then said I could have a doctor's report. The doctor said I shouldn't have to go to Scotland. Six months later I was sent another letter, saying this time I would go to the north of England to work in an office. A local councillor said that my own office job was of great importance to the war effort, and that was the end of that.

I started off in 1938 earning 25/- a week, which was a lot of money for a girl to earn then. In 1939 I earned £2 a week with 5/- stopped for income tax purposes. We never earned any overtime. I used to get an increase in my wages every year. It used to be about 5/- a year. In 1944 my wages were £3 10/- a week. I didn't get any specific rise because of the war. It was our bit for the war effort and that was that. The only time we were allowed any extra pay was one year, when we weren't allowed to have a fortnight's holiday. We could only have one week that year, and that had to be split up. You had to have Monday, Tuesday, Wednesday and six months later, Thursday, Friday, Saturday.

I was never shown the parts that I ordered, but a boyfriend who worked at the factory would bore me to pieces by taking his motorbike apart and putting it back. So I did know what a lot of pieces were for. During the war everything was coded and I know that we ordered parts for some of the floating docks that were used for the D-Day landings, but I had no idea what the parts were for. If you tried to find out anything you came up against a brick wall. We didn't talk about it, and we had passes with our photograph on it. The security was strict, but by the second half of the war it wasn't at all. I remember the slogans around the factory: "Be like Dad and Keep Mum."

I worked in the spares department on the Cardex system. My job was to keep a record of all spares that were ordered and sent out, so that when we got to below a certain figure, I would send the order department a docket to order some more.

We had a big table at the end of the office with the cardex system on it and I had three young girls working with me. They were anywhere from 14 years to 17 years old. Usually when they became 18 years old, they were called up, so I had to train some more. It was a tedious job continually entering up the orders and the dockets.

The Housewife — **What are her War aims** *on the Home Front this Winter !*

To Safeguard the Family against Ills and Chills

To Build up Strong Nerves

To maintain Energy for Work

To ensure Restorative Sleep every night

That is why she buys Ovaltine

P509A

The Nation's Protective & Nerve restoring Food Beverage

With the war the firm also made parts for aircraft and we'd have to keep a record of those as well.

There were a lot of motorcycles made during the war, but as far as the spare parts were concerned, the war department used to order them and it was colossal. Our orders came from the Ministry of Defence and it seemed to me that they used our firm for every blooming thing, because the amount of spares ordered far outweighed the machines that were on the road. Either they were rough with them, or the different units up and down the country didn't keep their records straight.

I know one particular airfield didn't keep their records straight, because a Sergeant was sent along to go through their lists with me, because it didn't tally with ours.

At the time there was a lot of air raids going on. When an air raid warning went, we would down everything and make for the shelter. We had to go through the spares office, down through the spares section into this underground place. It was rather hilarious, because this sergeant used to amaze us all; he used to be so frightened that, at the first bang, he used to go underneath the table. We used to say to him: "It's alright, its only an air raid warning."

We worked from 9am. till 6pm. and Saturdays from 9am. till 1pm. There was one time during the war when we had to work seven days on the trot. On the eighth day you'd have a day off. That never seemed to end. You never seemed to know what another department was doing. Everything was hush hush. And there was so much paper work, that on the eighth day the factory didn't close, because the other seven eighths of the work force would work that day while we were off.

I left my job at the motorcycle firm in 1944 because I was getting married.

After the war I wanted to get a job, because my husband was on poor pay, and I thought, we're not living from hand to mouth, so I got a job.

I worked for a cable company in their stock records department and I was talking to the men one day. They said to me: "When we came out of the forces there were women here doing our jobs." One man told me that the way he got his job back was by an elderly man who worked there saying to one of the women: "You know you're married and ought not to need a job, and all the time you're staying here the bloke, who used to do your job before the war is out of work."

That woman only worked another month and handed her notice in. The firm hadn't asked her to leave, the men did.

Pains I used to Dread

" I was keen to join one of the services but feared they wouldn't accept me. You see I knew I was subject to periodical pains which made me helpless while they lasted and I was afraid that even if I got in I should soon be turned out again as a 'wash-out.' I explained my trouble to a friend and she said at once ' those pains needn't stop you—simply get a box of A-K Tablets and take one or two in time. You'll be able to carry on without interruption. No depressing pain, no headache, no prostration.' I followed her advice and A-K are positively amazing." Get A-K Tablets to-day!

Service Industries.

Lily Jane

In the First World War I was working in a restaurant in the City. I was laying tables and seeing to the food. There were four or five nice girls working there, and I was over them. They didn't call me manageress, just helper. I used to get paid so much a week and then tips. I used to put a glass out, and the customers would leave money in that. When we'd finished, we'd share it. I like everybody to be the same, otherwise it causes a lot of dispute with people.

We used to serve fish pies, or roly-poly pudding, or bacon rolls. You'd make the pastry, roll it out take the rind off the bacon, lay it along the pastry, roll it up again, and when it comes out it's lovely. You could chop it in circles, with potatoes and greens. There were a lot of greens eaten in those days. You'd charge a couple of bob. Dinner was cheap then. We had to make the rations do for a week or a fortnight. When the dinner was over, and we had a quiet hour, then the food would arrive. I used to go with a couple of girls to collect it. When the customers had left, I'd tell the girls to wipe the tables and get them ready for the next person. We had to make sure they were clean, or we'd have the food inspectors round. When there was an air raid on, there was one room in the basement and we used to put the customers down there. They were allowed to stay there until the whistle blew.

I went dancing a lot, at the Elephant and Castle. There were plenty of boys there. I was blonde then, and I'd get stopped under the lights. They'd remember my hair. I'm easy to get along with if people are straight with me, but you've got to have a safeguard before you go intimate with men like that. If they turn rough, you've got no proof. I never went out with soldiers.

I was married in the Second World War, and I had a little boy. I would have liked to have joined the forces, but my mum didn't want me to go. I didn't want to upset my mum and dad. I wanted to do munitions work too, but dad wouldn't let me. He used to say, "There's others who can do that. You have plenty of work to do here." He was a bit strict.

Everything was chaos at first. My husband was called up, and you could ask to be evacuated if you wanted to, but I wouldn't leave mum and dad. I went to work part-time in a little tea place. It's a bit much for women, working all day and then coming home and having to do housework. When you get that seven days a week it's a lot. Someone used to look after my son when I was at work. She was a neighbour, and of course I paid her. You wouldn't expect her to do it for nothing.

The Second World War was a good time for women. I made a few bob. If you were a person who likes people and you didn't have a husband, well, that was when you could make friends with men. Men didn't like all these women working. On munitions the women would rush about getting extra money, and it would be more than the husband's. Some men would let them go to work, and some would say, "You're happy enough here. I give you enough money."

At the end of the war I thought, "Great, thank the Lord it's over." I looked forward to having a better life.

Alice.

In the First World War I was a cook, in Sheffield. I'm 94 now, and I was left a widow when I was 28. I had my husband's mother and my two children to feed, and I worked for us. I never asked anybody for a penny. My husband was a coach man on the railways. He had to help at night backing up the trains, and he was crushed between two of them. I was given an allowance of £5 a month, to keep me and my children, and my husband's mother. I went to work in the canteen of Boswell and Naylor's, the munitions factory, when the 1914 war broke out. My youngest girl was only two, and my boy was five.

I used to get there at 8 o'clock in the morning, and the first thing I did was make a vat of scones. The men would come in at 11 o'clock, and they used to have a buttered scone and a cup of tea, for 3 ha'pence. I did a good cooked dinner every day, and they'd have a sweet after. Their dinner was never more than six pence, and if they had a sweet it'd be a penny or tuppence more. Lamb chops were a penny a piece then, and pork chops were two pence. On Fridays I'd give them fish and parsely sauce, with mashed potatoes and peas, and I used to make bread and butter pudding for them. That used to be seven pence. In the afternoon they'd come and have another scone and a cup of tea. Chocolate was a ha'penny a bar, cigarettes five a penny, and ha'penny for a box of matches. Eggs then cost a shilling for twenty four; sugar was three pence ha'penny for two pounds; tea was four pence a quarter; best butter was eight pence, and you got two loaves for three pence ha'penny in those days. The meals were cheap because they were making ammunition. They lived and worked on the firm. I'll always remember, when the war was over, a dray came up the road with all the women on it, the bottle washers who worked at the brewery. There was one woman there who knew me, and she ran into the canteen, and said, "Alice, the war's over." I said, "That's a good job." Then old Mr Knott, the boss, he came down, and he said, "Turn your machines off and go home now. The war's over."

Before the Second World War I married again. My second husband worked in the munitions works, and we had a shop, a grocery shop. I used to bake bread and all sorts, and at one time I used to sell pies and peas at night in the shop when I was on my own.

We used to have sugar in sacks, and we'd weigh it up ourselves. When it was rationed it made it ever so difficult. I was soft, and I used to give people more than they should have, and then my ration would run out. I'd go to the suppliers, and they'd say, "You've had all your rations. You mustn't go over them," but they'd let me have some more. I used to feel sorry for people, and I'd lend them money for clothes and everything. The butcher's wife was a friend of mine, and I used to get a leg of pork on Fridays, and sell it with a big dish of stuffing. She used to say, "You can't afford stuffing with pork," but I've always been daft like that. It wasn't so much people going short of what they wanted, but that it was rationed. You had all except the quantity of it.

Marie Maberley

I came to England in 1939 because there were no prospects of getting work when you left school in Ireland. Even my father wasn't working. We were terribly hard up. My mother couldn't afford to keep us and if you wanted to earn any sort of a living then you had to do something. It was a hard thing to do at so young an age coming here to nobody. I managed to get a job in Birmingham.

I was doing hotel work, training to be a waitress. It was a dogs-body sort of job, running round fetching this that and the other. The wage was 5/- a week. We worked terrible hours for 5/- a week. You had your keep. You lived in. Your laundry was done. I guess they looked at the 5/- as pocket money. Out of that 5/- I would send my mother 3/-. I was working in the Grand Hotel in Birmingham when war was declared. It didn't alter the work in any way.

There weren't many clients staying in the hotel. but we had people coming in to lunches and teas.

Someone kept a check of how many people were in the hotel. We were given identity cards — I can still remember my number. It was — 1129QAZN and that was your identity card for a long while even after the war. You couldn't go anywhere without it. You had to show it, when you were asked. You got a ration book and of course you couldn't do anything without that.

We kept our clothing coupon book, but we gave up our ration book to the hotel.

I can remember being allowed two ounces of butter and once a month liver and bacon, if your butcher had it. There was black market. I couldn't be sure, but I think everybody had a hand in the black market. I think the hotel did. The meals altered in the hotel: You got a lot less, but for the guests they could get chicken and things like that, but at a price obviously. It was very unfair, that if you had money you could get what you wanted. I always felt that our boys — merchant seamen particularly — were risking their lives for people that made money out of it. I got a few pairs of stockings out of it, but I didn't think I was quite so bad. Our meals were basic in the hotel for us. We didn't get the extra, the guests did. We used to work seven days a week and have an afternoon off, or we'd have a morning off. You worked round the clock really.

The single people lived in. We had a dormitory with a half a dozen in the one room. It was in the basement, so it was rather grotty, and you shared the same bathroom and toilet. There were iron bedsteads and no luxuries. You couldn't complain to anyone, because you weren't in a union.

I felt cut off up there in Birmingham, because I didn't have many friends. I stuck it till 1940 and then I thought I'd come and stay with my sister in London for a while. When I first came to London I did housework. I saw a housework job in the paper one day, and thought that sounded not too bad. The house wasn't particularly big, and the people weren't posh either. I worked from about 10 o'clock till 4, and I earned £2 a week. I know felt rich. It seemed like a small fortune.

I would go off to the shelter if the siren went, although it very rarely went during the day. You didn't take so much notice of it in the daytime as you did at night. When I finished my housework job at 4 o'clock I'd go home and then we'd make our way down to our shelter. If you went to the pictures then you took the risk. When I lived with my sister we had a Morrison shelter and that was in the house. You slept in your clothes because you daren't get undressed in case you had to run out or were bombed. You had to be warm you see. You'd keep an old jumper and trousers to sleep in. You got into the Morrison because if the house fell on you the iron protected you. You felt safe. In the end I got more daring. We had a shelter in the back garden when I lived with my mother-in-law, but I just slept indoors.

Mabel Kibble

I worked over at the Civic restaurant, at Welling. I had to clean the hall and help with dinners and everything. There was a big sink where I used to wash up, and one day, when one of those doodle bugs came over, I dived under this sink. After that the manageress wrote, right across it, "This is Mabel's Hole," so I could go under there anytime.

After the air raids started I went in for fostering. I took on children from the Sidcup Homes. My own daughter was evacuated, but I got to be fed up and missed her, so I asked to take her back. My husband was in the army, on coastal anti-aircraft guns. I remember one day the water man knocked at my door. I knew him, because he lived along the road. I wanted something done with my taps, so he did it, and he said, "It's alright now. I'll give a look in tomorrow."

He came in next day, and he brought some strawberries from his garden. I said, "Oh, that's nice." He asked how were the taps, and I said they were alright, and then he said, "Do you go out in the week?" "Well," I said, "I never go out much. My husband's in the forces and I've got a daugther to look after."

Then he said, "You know, my wife don't understand me." They all say that. He said, "Would you like to come to the pictures with me?" I said "No, because my husband'd find out and I'd get into trouble." Blow me if he didn't knock next day! Well, I sent my daughter to the door and she told him my husband had come home on leave. They all tried it on.

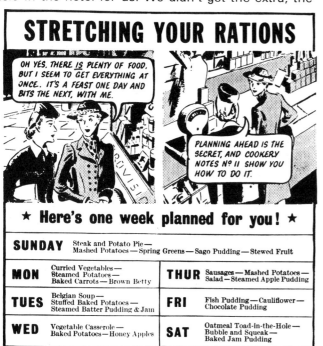

STRETCHING YOUR RATIONS

OH YES, THERE IS PLENTY OF FOOD, BUT I SEEM TO GET EVERYTHING AT ONCE.. IT'S A FEAST ONE DAY AND BITS THE NEXT, WITH ME.

PLANNING AHEAD IS THE SECRET, AND COOKERY NOTES Nº II SHOW YOU HOW TO DO IT.

★ Here's one week planned for you! ★

SUNDAY	Steak and Potato Pie— Mashed Potatoes — Spring Greens — Sago Pudding — Stewed Fruit		
MON	Curried Vegetables— Steamed Potatoes — Baked Carrots — Brown Betty	**THUR**	Sausages — Mashed Potatoes— Salad — Steamed Apple Pudding
TUES	Belgian Soup— Stuffed Baked Potatoes— Steamed Batter Pudding & Jam	**FRI**	Fish Pudding — Cauliflower— Chocolate Pudding
WED	Vegetable Casserole— Baked Potatoes — Honey Apples	**SAT**	Oatmeal Toad-in-the-Hole— Bubble and Squeak— Baked Jam Pudding

Lucy Apton

My first job on war work was way back in 1936, making gas masks. We used to sing while we worked. One day we were singing "London's Burning," and they heard us at the other end of the shop. The manager came in, and he said, "You, you, and you are fired." I don't know whether he thought I was the ringleader or what, but you got your cards and that was that. I was always in and out of work before the war. There was no union like now. No one would stick up for you. During the war I paid six pence a week to the engineering union. I went to a union meeting once, and the way they spoke sounded rather stupid to me. There was nothing about money or work, or anything like that.

Next I was directed to Vickers Armstrong's at Walton-on-Thames. I was compulsorily billetted. I'd been in and out of work so much, that to me it was just another job. I worked drilling parts of aeroplanes, and considering we were on war work, we didn't get very good money. But we never used to worry about money, as long as we were at work, and as long as we were earning. Men were drilling as well as women, but we weren't classed as men workers. We did a 48 hour week or more. I complained about the food we got on night work. The rice had bits of black in it, as if it had been swept up. I said the only thing to do was to go to the manager and refuse to work nights, if we didn't get proper food. The manager said, "I agree with you. If I speak to the cook and the food gets better, will it be alright? Will you work?" So I said yes.

At the end of the war I worked at Charing Cross. It was the "Dead End" of the war, when there wasn't so much bother with bombing. They asked me at the Labour Exchange if I would go as a ticket collector, and I thought it would be lovely. I had left the aeroplane factory because my husband said he wanted me to live at home. They always wanted to know your reasons for leaving a job. Before the war, when I left the gas mask factory, the woman interviewing me at the Labour Exchange wanted to know why I left, and I told her I had just left. I wasn't being cheeky, but she wrote a great big "NO" right across my card.

At Charing Cross they had girl guards, but not drivers. I collected tickets at the gates, but I didn't realise how much I would have to learn! You had to know all the figures on the trains that were coming in, so you knew where they were coming from, and you had to know all the different times. We only had a half hour for dinner, and I did get paid the same as the men, but railway workers were paid poor wages, so I was no better off than when I was earning as a woman worker. I was trained for six weeks on full pay. I was told to leave the railway at the end of the war. It was just another job I lost.

Mrs. Dudley

When I was in Teddington I worked on the railway at Strawberry Hill. I cleaned out the railway carriages. After I had my two children, I had a lady to look after them, so I could work. I used to do one week of days and one week of nights. When you were on nights you couldn't rest, because during the day you had to look after the children, and at night she'd look after them while you were working. I used to pay her. We had good money on the railway, because we had "danger money". I used to walk right across the electric lines while the bombs were dropping. If the siren went when we were cleaning the carriages out, the foreman used to come around and say, "Down quick!". The firemen used to teach us how to pull anybody out. We had one shelter and if we were lucky we got there, but if the warning was too short and they were right overhead, we would lie down under the seats. The fire bombs were the worst, because you couldn't hear them. When a bomb was going to drop it went quiet, and you knew you'd had it. The rescue teams and nurses and all that would come from nowhere.

He's been called up..

Please send only LIGHT PARCELS by Passenger Train

Heavy parcels cause delay and should go by GOODS Train

BRITISH RAILWAYS

G·W·R — L·M·S — L·N·E·R — S·R

Hilda Bennett

When I look back at the Second World War, I think it was the women who were the heroes, who worked, kept house, and had to fight every inch of the way for our weekly food. Boy, was it tough at times: you'd be lining up for fish, and just before it came to your turn, the fish you were going to buy for the evening meal was sold out. "Never mind," you'd say, "two herrings will do." If you can have something and you don't have it, that's your choice, but when you can't have anything, that's awful.

At the very beginning of the war, I was a sales lady, working in the Houndsditch Warehouse. It was a very beautiful white building then, with large pillars of glass in each department. I had to come up to London by workman's train. We were there by eight o'clock, and I didn't start work until nine, so we went into a church in Cannon Street and sat there and talked until it was time for work. At the end of the day, I used to get the bus to run me back to Poplar. I got off there and walked through the Blackwall Tunnel, all the way to where I lived, five days a week, and Sunday mornings too. When you got home, you'd have to eat your dinner in a hurry, and get changed because you were going in the shelter. You stayed in there till six in the morning, then you'd have a wash, take your sleeping gear off, and back to work.

My very first encounter with the enemy was coming home on a number ten bus as far as Poplar. Just before the stop, the driver must have had sixth sense, because he stopped very abruptly. A flying bomb was coming towards the stop we should have been on. There was an almighty bang, and a church near the bus stop was completely demolished. The whole of the top of the bus came off, and there was glass everywhere, but no one was injured. We all got off the bus white and shaking, crying and laughing at the same time, but not one passenger wanted to be taken to hospital, because we knew how busy they were with more important cases. We just went home, had a cup of tea with sugar, which I don't normally take, and forgot about it. We didn't talk about it.

Then I became pregnant and the bombs were dropping rather heavily, so the best thing my husband could do was find another place for us. He managed to get me somewhere to stay in Oxford. I had a very nice large bedroom in a house. The landlady was a lovely woman with a son of about eight years old. Her husband was a soldier, and he was away.

I tried to get work in a gown shop. I went there and had an interview. The woman said: "Yes, I can understand that you're quite a good sales lady, but I'm afraid you won't be very popular with the customers." I said, "Why not?" "Well," she said, "unfortunately the people in Oxford do not like Londoners." I was really shocked by this. I tried another few places and I got the same reply. There was a very large International Store there and it didn't matter where you were in the queue, the Londoners were always served last. That happened the whole time. I was disgusted.

But the person I was in digs with was wonderful. She couldn't have been better if she'd been my own mother.

Well, I was getting about 10/- a week from my husband and I couldn't manage on that, so as a last resort I tried for a job on the buses. They took me on, but it was horrible. I hated it, I really did. I had to get up at 4.30 in the morning in the winter. It was very very dark. I had to go over two big fields and cross a bridge and I was petrified. I used to hear a little bell tinkling, and I thought, my God, somebody's following me. It was quite some months before I found out that it was a dog going for a walk. I laugh about it now, but I didn't at the time. It used

This CONDUCTRESS says

"Journey breaks only give time for a hurried bite and up and down the stairs all day is trying. But 'Bisurated' Magnesia keeps me free of indigestion."

This reliable remedy for digestive upsets neutralises all excess acid in the stomach, and relieves the symptoms of indigestion. Ask your Chemist for 'Bisurated' Magnesia. 7d. to 2/10 (Incl Pur Tax)

'Bisurated' Magnesia

to take me an hour and a half to walk to work, and I got there at 6am.

I was a conductress. They gave me two or three days training, but no more. They were desperately short staffed. I stayed there till I was six and a half months pregnant. It was really hard going.

I had the baby in the Radcliffe Hospital. Soon after that I came back to London. My parents couldn't afford the fare to visit me as often as they wanted, so I lived with Mum in London through the rest of the war years and looked after my baby.

Irene

At the beginning of the Second World War I was just an ordinary housewife, with a six month old baby girl. In 1940 I lost my baby, and I had no other children, so it came that I had to do a job.

I went to the Labour Exchange, and they told me I'd have to do war work, so I put in for the post office. The nearest post office to me was the Mornington Crescent District Post Office, and it was quite a big one. You went to "school" in the post office, to learn where all the parts of London were. We were trained by postmen who were allotted the job, and we had to know each district of London because, not only were we postwomen, but we did a terrific amount of sorting as well. The postmen who used to take the little vans out collecting all the mail would bring it in, and it was tipped out on to this great big conveyer belt. At the end was a machine where a man would stand franking the letters, and then you would take them away and sort them into pigeon holes. We had what were called our walks, so we used to have to go and get our letters and sort them out into the different streets we were going to deliver them in. The walks were allotted in seniority. Some walks had much more to cart around than others, and some were quite small, especially when people evacuated from all around Regents Park and places like that. Our office was a walking distance from Euston Station and St Pancras Station, and also Kings Cross where they used to bomb.

We were definitely taking over men's jobs. When we post-women started, the men all belonged to a union and they didn't want women in there. Women had never worked in the post office, only behind the desk, as clerks, although there were some women there who'd been post-women in the First World War. Of course, they were married, and some had grand-children, and they came back to do the same work again in the Second War. There was money to be earned, you see. Some of the men were miserable to work for, but after a while they realised that the women had made a lot of difference to the atmosphere of the place. They thought they'd have to carry us, I suppose, and that we wouldn't be able to do the work. Naturally some people were better at it than others, and if they were very tiny, which some women were, they couldn't very well carry great big sacks on their backs. After a while the men realised that they had to take it, and they were quite good. They would be very helpful. In fact, quite a lot of people had romances, and got married and everything, from meeting in the post office. I was always afraid to have a romance, to be honest. There is a temptation, when you haven't seen your husband for years and years, but I always thought, if I do anything, something'll happen to him. I had my little crushes, naturally. I'd think, "He's rather nice, I hope I get put on a walk with him." Some of these older men were still nice.

Everybody had their own locker, and when we first went there, we were issued with boots, skirts, a jacket, and a hat with a big rim curled up. We got very cold, naturally, so after a while they let us have slacks. The uniform was navy blue, and it was a material more like a serge than anything. It was quite comfortable, I lived abut three miles from the post office, and when I was on night work I used to get the bus if it was running. Later on I got a bike and started to cycle. I had this lovely fur cape, which I exchanged for a cycle with a friend of mine.

After a while, when quite a lot of people had been called up, they wanted people to drive the post office vans. They asked me because I'd got long legs, and most of them who went in for it weren't tall enough. That was one thing I did regret, that I didn't take up the opportunity while I could.

When I was on night work, I'd be so tired once I got home, that I used to say to my sister, who was sharing a flat with me: "If there's a warning, don't wake me up, whatever you do." It was very upsetting for her, usually, if the warning did go, and now I think of it afterwards, I must have put her in a bit of a spot, but I had to get some sleep. It was quite long hours, from half past five in the afternoon to half past seven in the morning, and sorting all the time.

"FEMALE TEMPORARIES" AT WORK.

I was able to see these "temporary females" at work, in cramped positions behind pigeon-holes like egg-crates tipped sideways, operating stamping machines, or tying up mail-bags and filling in forms for the despatch. And this last part of their daily routine is perhaps the most difficult. After their five weeks course, in which they learn the elementaries of sorting (it takes years to make an efficient sorter) these girls find that the process becomes automatic and their speed and accuracy increases accordingly, but for "despatching" they become responsible for the safe arrival of everything from packages containing precious stones to seaside postcards.

For instance, on one bag there may have to be attached six different coloured tags which indicate its destination and to miss one from the bunch would mean that that delivery, instead of going to Kennington, might end up in Abbey Wood.

When I was on the Euston Road walk I often used to have to go into pubs, and all these American boys would be in there. "Here comes the mail lady," they'd say, "Got anything for me?" They always called you the mail lady, not post-woman, and it was rather embarrassing, going in there with this great big sack on your back. Sometimes, when you were delivering to blocks of flats you only had one letter for the top floor. Some of the post men would put a plank across from one building to the other, so instead of going all the way downstairs to get into the next block, you'd go up the top and walk over the plank. I thought I'd try it one day, up in Marylebone Road. You daren't look down, because it was very high, and did it once, but never again!

I remember one walk I went on when I was filling in for someone who was sick, where there was this man who had a registered letter delivered to him quite regularly. I think he was a bit of an invalid, because he was always in bed. He'd say, "come in," and then he'd get out of bed to sign for the letter, and he never had anything on. I'd been warned about him, and he must have done it deliberately. I was standing there thinking, "My God, let's get out of here!"

We had a lot of day light raids, and we used to have to stop work and go into the shelter downstairs. When I was on night work there were times when we never went upstairs at all, and all the sorting was done in the shelter. To start work at six o'clock in the morning I had to get up at five, and very often the warning would still be on. That wasn't very pleasant. I think the worst part of it was the blackout.

I was coming home from my mother's at about 10 o'clock one night, and there was such a bad fog that all the buses had stopped. There was a warning on as well, and you literally couldn't see a hand in front of your face. I was walking along the pavement, praying, "Let me get home, let me get home," when all of a sudden, this great big thing came rolling towards me. I thought, "My God, whatever is it?" Then this chap came running after it, and I realised it was a big drum. He said he was on his way to play somewhere, and it had fallen off his bike and come rolling towards me!

I must say that I enjoyed myself in the post office, and that is the truth. If you'd got to work, then I'm glad that I picked the post office. At the end of the war there were all these young blokes coming back, and there was a general feeling of a nice atmosphere. They never took any more women on, although I knew one woman who stayed on. You didn't have to leave, but once you did you weren't replaced by women. I left then to have my eldest son. I thought to myself, just as it's getting interesting I've got to leave to have him! But it was funny, once I knew I was having him, and when I had my other children, I never went out to work. My husband used to come home for lunch, so I couldn't go to work anyway if I'd wanted to. It was just one of those things that I thought I ought to do.

Patricia Graves

At the time war broke out, I had my own little touring repertory company. When war was declared, we were due to play in a place called Lyndale on the Yorkshire coast. Suddenly all the theatres were shut. I had a company of seven to eight people, men and women, just ordinary actors and actresses earning their living on a non-stop engagement. And this came as a bolt from the blue to everybody that our job and livelihood was finished.

Being an optimist, and having been a lifetime in the theatre, I never give up. So I said to the boys and girls, "Stand by for a fortnight and I'll guarantee your money, because I think that the country can't do without live entertainment." Well, everybody except one said, "Of course, we will stay." Most of them had been with me for two or three years doing West End plays, melodramas, full length plays and children's matinees.

We were due to play in the Town Hall in Lyndale — a very large building surrounded by ten and fifteen feet high windows, so with the blackout, this was a problem. I'd had the foresight to get yards and yards of black very wide material plus the materials to stick it onto the glass. So the first thing we did on the day we were shut down was to muck in and blackout the windows. Everyone got on with it and by the time the day was finished we'd done the whole building.

The next thing I had to do was go and see the Chief Constable of the Country of Yorkshire, so I set off for Guisborough at dawn. I had to get permission from him, you see, to open the town hall for theatre.

He was a charming man, but said: "I don't think there's any chance of you opening. Every theatre and cinema in the country is shut as you know. I'm certain that the Town Hall is a target for air raids, because you won't be able to black it out properly." I said to him: "Send anyone down anytime you like, I'm quite happy for you to inspect it." "I've a lot on my plate," he said, "so I can't have anymore of my time taken up, goodbye."

Well, every day I went to see him and he got so sick of me that he said: "Expect a man to visit you next week." I retorted: "I can't wait forever, I've had to have my hand in my pocket to pay the actors. Your money is guaranteed, mine isn't." "We'll see what we can do," he said.

When I went home to my digs there was a knock at my door and the landlady said: "There's a policeman at the door, miss." I went out to see this ruddy faced young constable.

"You've got a hall," he said, "that runs them there plays. Would you mind showing me where it is, because I can't find it." I showed him it saying: "There are the six steps, and if you ring, the caretaker will show you round. Goodbye." And I left him to it.

The next morning I raced round and the caretaker said to me: "I think you'll be O.K., because he was quite determined that there wasn't a hall there and I had to take him round and show him that there was. He couldn't see it!

I dashed to Guisborough and the Chief Constable said: "My constable couldn't find your hall, so I don't think the enemy planes will either. You can open tomorrow with your kids' matinee, but every child must carry a gas mask." I told him that I would do two children's matinees plus an evening performance. "Well," he said, "it mustn't go on after 9pm. and everybody must carry a gas mask." And that was it. We didn't look back from that moment. We did a different show every night and we went from strength to strength.

I continued this tour along the Yorkshire coast for several months, but then the men started getting called up and everyone started leaving. I didn't fancy the responsibilities of management any longer, so in the summer of 1940, I gave up the company and went to work for a friend in a little place outside Wolverhampton.

I fell to and was lending a hand with the sets, in fact I spent quite a lot of time up ladders with a hammer and nails! Being in the Midlands we were having nightly raids. The manager used to go in front of the curtain when a raid started and say to the audience: "You can go home if your homes are near enough to reach them in safety, or you can stay here. We shall continue the show if anyone wants to stay here and be entertained." Nine times out of ten, the audience stayed put. As for the actors, we were troupers. I only met one actor who was worried about the bombing. He literally shook in his shoes. When the announcement was made, he said: "We'll all go home now, won't we?" "Oh no," replied the manager, "You're under contract." So we played.

Eventually the company moved to a more safe area in Cumberland. There was plenty of food there and no raids.

During my time up there, I played many men's parts. I considered that to be my war effort. It was a great experience, I had a big voice and was very meticulous with my wardrobe. I took playing men's parts seriously and I was able to convince an audience, even in love scenes. I remember playing Charles in "Blithe Spirit" the leading man. The Cumberland area loved melodrama and blood and thunder, and we gave them their money's worth.

I had to go and register to do war work at one time, but the powers that be seemed to be quite happy with me acting. Keeping up the morale of the public! They told me: "You carry on, but you mustn't be out of work for more than a fortnight. If you change your job, you only get another job with a permit and that allows you to get work in your field within four weeks, or you will be sent to do some other work." Well, that never happened to me.

After three and a half years of touring, I decided to get a war job out of theatre. A friend advised me to go to see the Americans as they paid better than anyone else, so I went to the Head Quarters in Oxford Street and saw the Colonel, who, though I'd had no experience of any other work, thought he could fix me up with something.

I started off working in the medical records section which was housed in the annexe of Selfridges off Oxford Street. Everything was recorded in code, so instead of saying someone had a broken femur, you'd say "number twenty". You'd look up the code book to check everything. Well, working in theatre I found I could memorise the code book, so I got through the three weeks training in a week. I turned out more records a day than anyone else, because I didn't need to consult the book of words every five minutes.

After two months I was promoted to teaching the new entrants how to do this in record time. I said: "I can only teach them to work with their memories, but I can't give them a good memory if they haven't got one. So don't blame me if they can't remember anything! But train them in a week, I did! I found the work interesting and I stayed there about a year.

During that time we only had one calamity. We had a land mine, which hit the pub at the bottom of Duke Street and eleven of the boys were killed just as they were going on leave. It was very sad, because you knew them all. They used to give us chocolates, nylons and cigarettes and they were very good to us. That brought it all home to me and it saddened us all for a long time.

BOX OFFICE (A. J. DRISCOLL) Open 10 to 10 ... ... GERRARD 4506-7

Whilst smoking is permitted it is requested that it should be confined as far as possible to the intervals.

A.R.P. ————————————————————— A.R.P.

You will be notified from the Stage if an Air Raid Warning has been sounded during the performance—but that does not mean that an air raid will necessarily take place.

If you wish to leave for home or an official air raid shelter you are at liberty to do so. All we ask is that—if you feel you must go—you will depart quietly and without excitement.

The Nearest Air Raid Shelters are :
GOLDEN SQUARE (1 min., turning immediately right of theatre)
MOON'S GARAGE, Denman Street, (¼ min., turning immediately left of theatre)

A.R.P. ————————————————————— A.R.P.

In the interests of Public Health this Theatre is disinfected with Jeyes' Fluid

Health and Safety.

Vivian Prince

Well, I was in hospital in South-east London during the war, so you can imagine, it was pretty hectic. I worked in those days in what was known as the LCC, London County Council Health Service. One of the hospitals was at Lewisham, where I was quite a junior on the staff.

We used to try and help each other out, because in one area there might have been a pretty awful raid one night, and we used to go and help the staff, when they were overwrought with all the casualties that came in.

I was a radiographer and I do remember one case. There was a little boy of six and a small girl in another bed, whom I'd X-rayed. The little girl was unconscious, and we got her out of the rubble and she had multiple injuries, and she died. The poor little boy, his father, mother, brothers and sisters all died in that raid.

On one occasion I was wrongly identified on the slab. I was doing duty at Lewisham, and we had a raid. Some of the hospital was hit and someone of my height and build was found and people thought it was me. In fact I'd missed it, because I finished at 8am., had breakfast and went off. Next day when I went back on duty people looked at me as if they'd seen a ghost. They thought they had to break some terrible news to my parents. That was the time they were the nicest to me ever!

I had one or two adventures getting to hospital and back. I remember having to go to a hospital, which was the other side of Blackwall Tunnel, and I waited and waited for a bus to get me back, and suddenly a man came along on a horse and cart, with a little girl. He stopped and said: "Are you going through the tunnel?" I said: "I'm hoping to." "Well," he said, "if you don't mind getting on the back of this horse and cart, we'll take you through the tunnel." So there was me sitting on the back of this horse and cart.

Another time I'd got to Blackheath Station and the sirens went, and we had a horse cab which came across Blackheath and was actually stabled at the top of Kidbrooke Park Road where I lived. I knew the cabby by sight, and every time a raid started, he'd take the horse

and cab back to the stables. He saw me and said: "If you don't mind risking it miss, would you like me to give you a lift?" Well we got to the middle of the heath, and I can assure you that the raiders were overhead, and the horse went mad because the mobile gun on the heath started up. Well I just thought, "Here we go. This is the end of me." The horse started making these terrible panting noises, and I thought, "It's going to drop dead". Well my mother heard this terrible noise coming up the road, and it stopped and her daughter gets out of this cab. "Well," she said to me, "don't you ever do that again." I thought, "I'm not going to!"

There was a lot of give and take during the war. We didn't have any trade union shifts or anything. If somebody'd been off sick, you tried to double up. We weren't fussy. We'd got a war to win and that was all there was about it. If I was on all night I'd finish at 8am. There was a team of us, all women except for one old man, Wilf. He was marvellous. He was an absolute scream of a man and used to reside across the road, I think it was the George public house. Whenever Wilf was missing, we knew where to get him, in the George.

When war was declared a lot of the fever hospitals were cleared out, and we had a certain amount of beds in those hospitals. We took some of our patients there. They were crowded if you had a terrible raid. For instance, there was a terrible raid in Lewisham, in front of the shops, Woolworths and Marks & Spencers. There used to be a bit of grass in front and now if you look, it's all concreted over. So many people were killed that they had to concrete it over.

I remember my father died in 1941 and we'd had some bad raids. The police came to tell my mother that he'd had this terrible stroke, so we had to get over there. He died the next day and my brother went to arrange the funeral and he said: "Well I know we queue for an awful lot of things, but I've never had to queue for a funeral before." There were so many people needing attention, that he had to queue half way round Lewisham to get into the undertakers.

Mrs. Bancroft

When the Second World War broke out, my husband and I had a shop at Herne Hill, but he got called up and rushed over to France, so I was left with the shop on my own. I decided to sell the shop and join the ambulance service. I had driven a van for the Arsenal in the First World War, so I thought I could do it in the Second.

My ambulance station was on the top of Knights Hill. At first a lot of young fellows and girls with scarves round their necks, and driving sports cars and the like, volunteered. They soon fizzled out. I don't know where they went.

Anyway, we were based in a garage at Knights Hill at first, and when the raids were on, all we had was a sort of glass thing joined on to the garage, and we had a few deck chairs to sleep in. In the mornings you'd feel around for the glass and say: "Are the windows still in?" Eventually they got us a big house with a basement and four floors, so we were well away then. We covered Crystal Palace, Brixton everywhere, and Brixton was always alight.

We'd wait in the house for calls. There were four of us girls, two on each shift. We'd be on all night and then come back and have breakfast.

We had to have first aid lessons, although all I wanted to do was drive, but I passed my first aid certificate.

When we first joined we had a cotton coat, a cotton blouse, a tie and a cotton hat plus one pair of shoes. That's all. It was about a year before we got any thicker clothing. In the meantime this girl and I went up to London and had our own uniforms made. We put London Auxilliary Ambulance Service on our uniforms and people used to wonder who we were! When we did get our uniforms, the first night I had mine on, I was just going on at night and the raid started. You were supposed to get down in the gutters, but I thought, not on your nelly, not in my new uniform!

Our ambulances weren't like they are now. They were completely empty. They just had two runners this side and two runners that side, and you would run the stretcher on to it and get to the hospital as quickly as you could. There was no medical equipment in the vans.

The girl who was with me in my van was a gold medallist in first aid, and when we'd get to an incident, she tended to run off and do her own thing. Well, of course, you weren't supposed to do that! We were to wait till the heavies, the auxilliary services, got people out. We were supposed to stay with our van. She used to disappear and I'd have to take them to hospital by myself. We were supposed to put labels on them, saying what was wrong with them and so forth, but you didn't have time. You got them there as quick as you could.

You were supposed to bring back your stretchers and blankets, no matter what state they were in. One night at Dulwich Hospital all the dental department, medical department, every department was full of stretchers, so all I could do was leave my cases on the floor, because I needed the stretchers and blankets.

We were supposed to stick to the rules and work in certain areas. One night you'd be in district 1, the next district 2 and so on. If you weren't on your right list, then you put everyone else out. One girl was given permission to go and pick up anywhere she liked, because she would not stick to the rules. She couldn't see that she put us all out.

We got paid £3 a week for our work, and we did have some men who volunteered to work on days they weren't working, but at nights it was very difficult to get them out. The nurse who went out to deliver babies, could demand a car from us anytime. One night I was out all night when the raid was on, and they never asked me into the house. The baby wasn't born till the morning, and when the nurse came out she said: "I'm going to report those men, it's always you women who come out. The men, either they're ill or it's something else." The men always made excuses not to go out with the nurse. One man used to volunteer and he'd shake so much when the raid was on, that our chief used to push him under the table in the kitchen and leave him there.

One night we were called to Brixton, and I had a man with me this time. One of the wardens had a fire bomb dropped right in front of him and he was blinded. In order to get him to hospital we had to go under this bridge. Well, the man said to me: "I'm not taking this ambulance under that bridge with all these fire bombs dropping." I said: "Well, what are you going to do then?" He stayed behind and I had to drive the ambulance myself to the hospital.

Some of the men I met, they were really cowards.

The heavies worked really hard. I remember one night we were called out to a big house, and the whole of the back of this house had been split down the back like a doll's house. There was an old woman up on the top floor in bed. Her bed was on a ledge, just one piece of wood, and the man had to creep along to get her out. He had to hold her and get her along and then all down the stairs. When he got her out the first thing she said was: "You haven't brought my slippers."

In our spare time we were supposed to rest, when we had twenty-four hours off. The girl who was with me, the gold medallist in first aid, she would go round hunting for people in the ruins. She was very zealous. One day we went to Crystal Palace and she got right up the top of a building, and feeling about amongst the ruins, she felt something like bone. She pulled it out, and it was an old man's bald head. I said to her: "Serve you jolly well right. You shouldn't go in your spare time. You're supposed to rest."

You had to see the funny side of things.

Siege Cake

4oz dripping or lard
4oz moist sugar
4oz golden syrup
1½ teacupsful buttermilk
lemon flavouring
1 level teaspoon bicarbonate of soda
12oz flour

NB To save sugar 6oz of syrup and 2oz of sugar can be used. If buttermilk is not available use ordinary milk, 1 level teaspoon of cream of tartar, and ½ teaspoon bicarbonate of soda.

Grease a cake-tin measuring about 7 inches in diameter. Beat fat, sugar and golden syrup until the consistency of whipped cream, gradually work in the buttermilk. Sift the flour with bicarbonate of soda and work it lightly into the mixture. Add the lemon flavouring. Bake in a moderate oven for about 1¼ hours.

Ivy Jones

At the factory where I worked, we had to do firewatching. I think it was the law. Every person over 18, including girls, would have to do firewatching. There was a rota and you couldn't get out of it, but if you had a husband home on leave, you could have that week off and the rota would be changed.

The men who did the firewatching didn't mind us. In fact it was the first time I knew men outside my group of sisters and friends.

I can remember meeting this chap from Manchester and he wanted to take me home to meet his parents, and it was like going to America! His parents had to write to my mother, and even then she didn't believe it, and wanted to write to his commanding officer to find out if he really came from there!

Before the war you didn't get a lot of married women working. When the war came, suddenly married women were being able to work. For the first time I was working with women over twenty. We were happy working. I don't think we went back to the fireside in the same way again.

I was frightened doing fire watching, but after a while I shut my mind to it and hoped it wouldn't happen to me.

We always had a fireman in charge when we did firewatching. They taught us how to put our helmets on and how to do it quickly. We wore heavy boots and protective clothing. It was the first time I ever wore slacks. They were green corduroy and zipped on the side. My mother thought they were really disgusting, because I looked too boyish.

NO "OFF DAYS" NOW!

"JUST TAKE TWO A.K. TABLETS AND YOUR PAINS WILL GO IN FIVE MINUTES."

If periodical indisposition for you means unbearable headaches and depressing pains, you will find an unfailing remedy in "Anti-Kamnia." At the first symptom of pain take one or two tablets. The suffering you dread will pass you by and you will be fit and able to carry on with your work and keep all your engagements as usual. Almost the moment you take "Anti-Kamnia" you get relief, headache vanishes, pain disappears and your nerves become soothed and calm. "Anti-Kamnia" is the remedy prescribed by physicians and recommended by nurses, because of its wonderful power to relieve pain and the fact that it does not disturb the natural action of the female system in the slightest. Why not get the tablets today and have them in readiness.

Anti-Kamnia
BRAND ANALGESIC TABLETS
AK ALWAYS SURE-ALWAYS SAFE

Thousands of women simply ask for A-K. If you say A-K your chemist will know. 1/5 a box (Including Tax).

FIREWOMEN PLAY THEIR PART.

Despatch Rider Commended.

While deserved praise is bestowed upon firemen for their swift and effective assistance at fly-bomb incidents, appreciation must also be shown to the women of the N.F.S. Firewomen are putting in meritorious work —and not always behind the scenes.

At every station, from the nerve-centre at Fire Force Headquarters to the tiny outpost station in Southern England, firewomen are playing their part. At each mobilising and control room, at each watchroom, canteen and kitchen, in administrative offices, on motorcycles and on the spot at incidents, you will see firewomen at work. Trained for their job, they toil at their various posts during day and night, helping the civil defence organisation to minimise the effect of Hitler's latest weapon.

In addition to their service duties, the women of the N.F.S. render much appreciated assistance at nurseries and rest centres. If a centre is in urgent need of a telephonist through sickness or any other cause a trained firewoman is always ready to fill the gap. At rest centres firewomen lend a ready hand at preparing tables for meals, washing up, finding billets for the homeless, and generally assisting the overworked staff. At a day nursery firewomen occasionally assist in bathing the babies, while at another rest centre a firewoman typist assists in the administrative work.

When a flying bomb dropped near a fire station recently the women hurried from their quarters to assist in rescue work and first-aid. A fire station was recently badly damaged by blast. Several of the female staff sustained cuts and shock. When arrangements were being made for their evacuation to another station they pleaded with their Group Officer to be allowed to remain and help the men clean up the mess. They stayed on.

"MARSHY" THE CHEERFUL.

At almost every N.F.S. station will be found new pets—cats, in particular, rescued from bombed buildings by firemen, and now being cared for by firewomen until new homes can be found for them.

Firewoman Despatch Rider Marsh has been commended by the Fire Force Commander for "meritorious service and outstanding devotion to duty while attending fly-bomb incidents since the commencement of this form of enemy action." Day or night, at a given signal, Despatch Rider Marsh dons her top boots, crash helmet and goggles, mounts her motor-cycle and is away in a flash to the scene of the incident. Her job is to act as courier to the Assistant Fire Force Commander, but Miss Marsh finds plenty to do besides. As soon as she is free from her official job she rushes away to assist the rescuers. From her satchel slung over her shoulder she slips out her first-aid kit and sets to work bandaging the wounds of the injured.

All the rescue workers know "Marshy," the tall, pale-faced and ever-smiling N.F.S. despatch rider. Her constant cheerfulness and good spirits help others in their work, and have a tonic ecect on bomb-shocked and homeless men, women and children. At one incident she entered a room in which bombed-out people were awaiting a conveyance to the rest centre. Holding up a bandage, she said. "Doesn't anyone here need bandaging? This is my last one and I am not going to take it back." Instantly there were smiles.

Miss Gladys Marsh likes the Fire Service and motor-cycling, but best of all she likes first-aid work. "I always wanted to be a nurse," she told a reporter.

Fusilier Derrick Bruce Smith, youngest son of Mr. and Mrs. F. R. Smith, 92, Brinklow crescent, Shooters Hill, has been killed in action in Normandy.

There were twenty-four of us on duty at one time. We'd be split into groups and work with the men. We did two hours on and two hours off.

I can remember when we first learned to hold the hose. It was hilarious, because the five of us went flat on our faces. It did take more women to hold the hose, but we did it, and we also learned how to use the stirrup pump for emergencies, like incendiary bombs.

The one thing we weren't allowed to do was to be right on the top of the buildings and we could only climb the ladder a certain height.

When we finished our turn we'd go to the air raid bunks and wake up the others to go on duty. These shelters were like bedrooms and it became like a club down there. We'd have a wash before starting work at 8am and we'd get a breakfast in the canteen of dried eggs or spam.

Sylvia Jacobs

It was 1942, when I came into the rest centres. I wanted to do something helping people. I could never have joined the forces. I always had pacifist views. I didn't belong to the Peace Pledge Union, but I definitely was determined that I wouldn't do anything to kill people. My time in the war would be to try and help people who were suffering from it. In some respects I saw more action in the rest centres than I would have done, if I'd been sent to some remote part of England to be a typist in some forces office.

At that time the rest centres were run by the old Poor Law department of the London County Council. I was in Area 6, which covered Hammersmith, Kensington, Paddington and Chelsea.

The idea was to have places, where the people who had been bombed out of their homes could go to immediately. They came to us before they went back to their homes, if they had to be found alternative accommodation, or if they had to leave London altogether.

At the very beginning of the war there was an idea that there wouldn't be this necessity. They assumed everybody would be killed. We were told very early on that the L.C.C had provided hundreds and hundreds of papier-mache coffins for the remains of people, but that they had not provided for people who would be alive. It was only after the blitz and the fire of London they realized there were actual survivors, so schools were taken over to be run purely for this, although during the day and when there wasn't any bombing, children went there and we provided them with meals and looked after them.

When I first joined the rest centre, I was a washer-upper and cleaner-upper and then graduated to being a welfare adviser.

The staff at the centres consisted of a manager, deputy manager two welfare advisors, who alternated, a nurse and general assistants, who helped provide meals, clean up and do odd jobs.

I worked 24 hours on and 24 hours off and when there wasn't any population — that is bombed out population in the centre, I could have a few hours sleep in my office. The population slept on bunk beds in the actual classrooms.

I used to get £2/10- per week plus subsistence allowance of 3/- a day, when there was no population. You lost it when there was population, because it was assumed you'd eat what was provided for the population.

My actual job was receiving people who had been bombed out, perhaps concentrating a little on the flying bomb people. Some of them were just carried in, in blankets. They'd lost their clothes and were absolutely black from the dust, and bemused, because they had no idea what was happening.

I'd record them coming in, find out if there was anywhere for them to go, send them to places for clothes, money or rehousing.

One night during the fire bomb attacks, I went to three rest centres in one night. They came and collected me. I took in one hundred people in one, then moved on to another and at 7am I was taken somewhere else. The officer, who brought me along suddenly looked at me accusingly, saying: "You look tired." "No", I said, "I'm not tired". I'd been working for 24 hours.

There was a lot of pure comforting to do. I used to find in the evenings, with people coming home from work, or their rounds of all the authorities, they'd just, come and

sit and talk. I'd spend from 6pm to midnight just talking. Even after people found their own homes again, or new ones, they'd still come and talk. They felt safer in the centres because of all the people.

A lot of houses were requisitioned, so that people who had lost their homes could be found alternative accommodation. I remember a remarkable little woman of 4ft. 10in. She and her sister, her 7 year old child, and husband, who was dying of Parkinsons disease were bombed out and came to me. One day she came in very excited saying: "Isn't it marvellous, there's a requisitioned house in Riverside Walk. My husband has always longed to live there, and they're offering it to us."

It was rather an upper class area, so someone thought better of it and the next thing she knew she was told: "It will take a long time, so we'll offer you something else." I said: "No don't worry, you can stay here as long as it takes." So she did. One of the neighbours in Riverside Walk was extremely objectionable to the family when they first moved in and the woman complained about it. Well, I started working on that, but I needn't have done, because it was sorted out later and then it was the neighbour, who was asking protection from the 4 ft. 10 in. woman!

I remember particularly, when an old people's home was bombed out. It was run by a Catholic society and what was so upsetting about it was that it was full of old men and they'd never been so happy in their lives, as when they were bombed out, because they had a freer life and lovely meals and one man, who was the "head boy" we called him, he always used to make a speech to the cook. She had to come in and be congratulated on her meals.

We had to train them, while they were there not to always make their beds and pack everything up at night, which they'd been forced to do. We all bade them farewell very sadly, when they had to go back to the convent.

Later on they were looking for people to work in rest homes for the aged and the infirm and I got a job there.

For women it was marvellous that they could get away from home, but more so for the upper middle class families, where the daughter was stuck at home till she married. There were tremendous opportunities for women in that way, but probably more so for the upper classes. A friend of mine was lecturing to two women's guilds, and he was talking about women going out to work and not going out to work. These women looked at him in utter amazement and said: "But we've always gone out to work. We had to, we couldn't have kept our families without."

We forget about those women who were doing dreary jobs, with terrible pay, but they always knew they had to work, so for them the war wasn't so different, but gave them the opportunity for better pay.

Many women had to bring their families up on their own, with husbands away for years and under difficult circumstances. Those women had to be very independent indeed.

My end of the war was hospital. I was carried out feet first from my rest home for old people and taken to Hackney Hospital. I spent 7 weeks there with chest trouble and was then sent down to a special unit in the country. I was a whole year off work.

Ellen.

I joined the Red Cross before the war, and I became a cadet officer. When war broke out I was training cadets. They were eleven years old to thirteen, and I was training them to join the St. John's Ambulance when they were older.

One day there was a day light raid at a school in Catford, and some children got killed. Their monument is up at Hitler Green Cemetery. We had to finish with the cadets then, because a lot of them were sent away.

I used to leave work at five and get my uniform and go straight down to London Bridge. That was our first job when the raids started, to go to London Bridge, under the arches to the shelters. All the down and outs were there. They had nowhere else to go when the war started. We also went into the crypt at St. Martins. We used to do all their feet, and they were in such a bad state. At first the shelters were only the arches of London Bridge and not just down and outs but local people would go there. London Bridge was, well you had to see to believe. Nothing had been organised. We had to look after the people, if they had diabetes or any complaint, we looked after them. Later a canteen was there and bunks for children to sleep on.

One day I came home, in the morning, and our house had been bombed. I had to take my mother and leave the house as it was. A lot of things got stolen, we had to start again. Our house was patched up and I went back there. Mum went off to Wales with my sister.

If the Red Cross wanted any help, they would send somebody to the shelter, or else we went to the headquarters. If we were called to the scene of a raid, we would do first aid. We'd comfort people and do simple first aid till the ambulance came to take them to hospital. I used to do this seven days a week. It's surprising how much energy you've got really. I don't remember sleeping at night in the shelters. If it was a quiet night you might get a sleep, and in the morning you had to do all the injections for the people who were diabetic.

When you think about what we all went through and what it is now, you wonder why you did it all. I did it and never thought about it. I just did it. I could have got in the Land Army and got away from it all. After the war I got a letter from the Queen thanking me for all the services rendered in the Red Cross.

WHAT CAN I DO?

From the point of view of the Stay-at-Home Housewife.

BY the time you read this we shall have grown used to air-raid warnings and black-out nights; that is to say, we shall have adapted ourselves to the changed circumstances and be engaged in the important business of "carrying-on" as best we can, making the best of our war conditions for ourselves and those around us.

An unspectacular job, compared with the various public activities involving uniforms and a feeling of national importance, but absolutely essential to the life of the nation; to live as normally as possible under difficult and altered circumstances is the very essence of sanity in a crazy world.

In times of crisis the vital necessity is for us all to keep our heads, not panic; when the disaster is on us, the important thing is to "carry-on" calmly, philosophically, and as near to normally as possible.

Appalled by the enormity of the disaster, the ordinary non-political, non-professional woman, pre-occupied with her home and family, asks herself, What can *I* do?

43

Mrs Smith

The year before war broke out the A.R.P. came into operation. I volunteered at that time to become a part-time Air Raid Warden.

As a part-time warden I didn't have a uniform as such. I was given protective clothing, it was like water-proof clothing really, leggings and a jacket. I had an arm band with A.R.P. on it, and I had a whistle and a rattle.

The whistle was for me to blow in case I needed any help and the other warden would hear it and come to help. The rattle was in case of gas attacks. I was also given a proper regulation gas mask and helmet like the forces were issued with.

They gave me nothing for my feet. Seems silly to give you waterproof clothing and nothing for your feet.

As a volunteer I didn't get paid anything, but the full-time wardens did. I used to work one night on and one night off. I started at 8pm. at night and finished at 6am. next morning. Don't forget that I had to go to work the next day as well. Nobody ever said to you that because you were on night duty the day before you could have the day off!

I was stationed in a brick operations room with a telephone at Burrage Road School in Plumstead. There was two way walkie-talkie as well. The room was like a bunker above ground 8ft by 8ft. There was a couch and a heater and something for us to make tea and coffee, although we provided it ourselves.

There was four of us, two part-timers and two full-timers. The full-timers worked twenty-four hours on, and twenty-four hours off. They'd start at 8pm. one night and finish at 8pm. the next night. The didn't have to stay awake the whole time and someone didn't always have to be in the bunker in the day time, but at night there was more chance of an air raid, so then someone did.

My job was to walk up and down streets in the blackout looking for any bombs that might be dropped, people in trouble, or anything that looked suspicious. I covered about twenty-four to thirty streets and it was a neighbourhood thing really, because everyone knew who the wardens were. During an air raid I was allowed to find some cover, but really you had to be round and about and if you heard anything drop you had to be able to locate it quickly, so you could send a message.

I would report at 8pm. the night I was on and the full-time warden would ring to the operational centre, telling them that she now had her part-timer. I would then go on my round. One warden had to stay in the bunker to look after the telephone. Sometimes I did, sometimes the full-time warden would stay there.

When the war first started, I ducked for every little sound if I was outdoors or in. After a while I got so used to the noise that I knew if it was near or far. If a bomb dropped a good way away you'd feel a jar, but if it was in the next street you'd get a broken glass and feel as if the building had been picked up and put down again. It's a thing you've got to live through, before you can really understand it.

When a bomb dropped and I was on duty, I had to locate it as quickly as I could. It didn't take long, because I would see the cloud of dust and someone would be running to locate the warden and tell us about it. I would either run to the bunker myself, or get someone else to go there, while I went to where the bomb dropped. The warden on duty in the bunker would then phone to operational headquarters and they would send the fire brigade and ambulance service, and the police.

Having got to the incident, I would then have to organise things until the services arrived. You always found that if anything happened a crowd of people would come from nowhere and offer to help. I was taught first aid, so I would help people where I could, and comfort them until the ambulances could arrive. We

NOTICE # HI 388423

1. **Always carry your Identity Card.** You may be required to produce it on demand by a Police Officer in uniform or member of H.M. Armed Forces in uniform on duty.

2. **You are responsible for this Card, and must not part with it to any other person.** You must report at once to the local National Registration Office if it is lost, destroyed, damaged or defaced.

3. If you find a lost Identity Card or have in your possession a Card not belonging to yourself or anyone in your charge you must hand it in at once at a Police Station or National Registration Office.

4. Any breach of these requirements is an offence punishable by a fine or imprisonment or both.

FOR AUTHORISED ENDORSEMENTS ONLY

were taught at our first training that, if at all possible, we should not give people food and drink. Forget about brandy and tea. That person might look alright on the outside, but internally be in a bad way. I was very strict about this and I was often called a "little bitch" or "cow" over it.

I had to stay at my post until everyone was out and seen to in case any next of kin had to be notified. I had to make out a report for the operational centre, which would be telephoned through. The report had where the incident was, the time, and how long it took the auxillary services to get there. I put down how many houses were damaged, how many people were in the houses and if they were alive or dead. I also put down which hospital they went to.

I remember once in Vincent Road a direct bomb fell onto some houses there. I can remember feeling very sick, because I was helping to get people out and I came across a headless body. I don't know who the person was but it was the head of a woman, and I turned round and was violently sick.

During the war we tried to live as normal a life as possible. Some people got to the stage where they didn't want to know about air raid shelters. Air raid shelters themselves received direct hits and in my area there weren't enough shelters anyway. They were stuffy and there was no privacy, and we know what married people get up to! We tried to live as normal a life as we could in

our own homes.

Social life was difficult during the war. All cinemas and theatres were closed to start off with. They opened up a few months later. There used to be loads of cinemas in Woolwich, the Odeon, Granada, Hippodrome, Premiere. I remember my Mum and I going into London to see "Gone With The Wind", and how we got there I don't know, because there was a big incendiary raid the night before. It took us about four hours to get up there, because from Woolwich to Charing Cross it was all criss-cross with burning buildings, hoses, fire engines, the lot. It was a tremendous detour, but to us it was our only social life.

One night a crowd of us, three boys and three girls, had been to the Embassy dance hall at Welling, and at about 1am. we were going home and everything was coming down. There were no buses and no trams and and the bombs were falling, incendiaries, shrapnel, everything in the way of a bombardment was being chucked down. We couldn't find a shelter, and we were all a bit drunk, so we started dancing, waltzing, foxtrotting and singing. Suddenly this policeman came out of this side turning and said: "Be quiet, you are causing a public nuisance." It seemed funny considering the noise all around us, but we did go home quietly chatting. We were frightened, but we had to have our social life. It wasn't much fun in the Anderson shelther, or under the table!

Rose Martin

I decided to take in neighbours' children, so the women could go on war work. They were mostly working on small arms in a factory, which was on the Rochester Way.

The children were dropped off at my house at about 9 o'clock in the morning and collected at lunchtime. After lunch there would be two or three more, for the mums who went in the afternoon session. This was all voluntary, because people felt it was part of their effort to help the war.

I thoroughly enjoyed it, because my children had the company of other children, in the care and safety of myself. I had a shelter outside the house, where I would marshal them in the event of an air raid, and the mums would be able to work, knowing there was someone with their children.

I wasn't the only mum. There were several mums and it was nothing to see two or three mums marshalling the children out of the house into the shelter.

A child was always encouraged to pick up one toy, whichever was nearest, and then if they were in the garden, we used to hear the warning go, because in our road one of the houses had been commandeered for the ATS. They used to get the warning before we did. We used to hear their alarm go, so we didn't wait for the public alarm. The minute I heard their buzzer go, that was an indication to get the children ready, and pick up their toy or their book, or whichever they wanted. They walked out hand in hand into the shelter.

Some of them, even though they were only five, were aware of what it was all about.

I was very happy doing that with the neighbours. I also got very interested in the Soldiers and Sailors Families Association, which did a lot of war work. A lot of us mums had husbands in the forces and a lot of us were helped considerably, especially if we were bombed, which I was.

We had wonderful bundles of clothes given us, which were sent from America. They were beautifully made, brand new clothes. You'd have trousers, shirts and coats, shoes and socks for a boy, or dresses, socks, underwear and shoes for a girl. Usually in these bundles was a note or a letter from the donor in America. In the bundle I received, the time that I was bombed, was a note from a teacher in Illinois. She had a class of twenty-four pupils and every one of those children had written a note inside, a little scrap. What amused us was the names. Paddy Asper, Norma Kipper, names I remember well. I kept in contact with her for a long time.

When I was evacuated with my mother to Bideford, we were met at Waterloo Station and were escorted there. We were on a troop train, which had a lot of American soldiers who were going down to camp. They very generously gave us their lunch boxes, because we'd had no food and there were no buffet cars on the trains.

The journey started at half past seven from Waterloo and we did not arrive in Bideford until five o'clock that night. Most of us were from Greenwich, New Cross, Charlton or Kidbrooke.

From the station we were then transported to the little village into the church hall. It had already been made known to us what families we were going to, and I went to a farmer and his wife, who was already housing my brother as an evacuee.

She had a spare bedroom, and she had a dairy, which she wasn't using. We could use the dairy as our living room, and we had the bedroom. The two children had iron cots, and my mother and I shared the bed, and then our living room was the dairy. There was no lighting, but oil lamps, which took a lot of getting used to, especially after you'd been used to switching on electric light. They had to be trimmed every day and the wicks trimmed, and filled up with parafin. Light cooking was done on the fire grate in our dairy but Mrs Roe, who owned the house, used to allow my mother and me to use her kitchen range two days a week, so we would have a bake up.

The rationing wasn't so strict, as in London. In the meat range we could get brawn, offal, liver and kidneys. Milk was plentiful, so we weren't rationed and as for eggs, the children used to delight in going out and getting them from the hedges, where they were free range chickens. My children knew what it was to go out and pick up a nice warm brown egg. The Christmas we spent there we had a marvellous pork dinner. We thought about the poor people in London. They probably got one rasher of bacon.

They did put themselves out for the London evacuees. It was difficult at first, especially when the children went to school. There the schools are open classrooms and the teachers had to cope somehow with the influx of evacuee children.

I came back against my mother's wishes. She came

NORMA KNIGHT *wants you to meet* . . .

Mrs. John, who gives her neighbour a helping hand

my next door neighbour goes out to work

1 . . *so I do her daily shopping and cook her evening meal with mine. It's no harder cooking for six than for four in my opinion.*

2 *After the meal she and her husband do the washing up. It's a very good arrangement because it gets everything cleared away early.*

The gentle lather of Knight's Castile gets right into the pores, removes all grime and wonderfully refreshes the skin.

Knight's Castile

PREVENTS 'TIRED SKIN'

KC 286-396-100

3 *Shopping is fun too. By pooling our meat coupons we make shopping easier. And we find we have much in common. For instance, we both use Knight's Castile. It's a grand soap for keeping the skin smooth and clear.*

JOHN KNIGHT, LIMITED — SOAP MAKERS SINCE 1810

back to bury my grandfather, and she begged me not to come back. I was very tempted, in as much as I knew my house had been completed of repairs. It was what they called First Aid repairs. The house became habitable, according to the London County Council. That was a great temptation to come back, which I did.

During the war people talked so much more. There was not the silent reserve you sometimes get if you sit in a railway carriage, or if you're shopping. I think queues did a lot for that. Every time you went for your rations, or you made your daily or weekly trip to the shops to pick the rations up for the week, you could be up to two or three hours in a queue, and people talked. They would relay their experiences of a raid, or talk about food, and different things you could do with making the rations stretch.

You had three types of ration books, buff book for an adult, a blue book for a child aged five and over, and a green book for a baby. A green book was always the priority book, so that if bananas, eggs, oranges, or anything like that came in, you got preference on the green book.

The first time I had bananas, when I brought them home, the children looked with horror first of all, not having seen them for so long, and when I peeled them, they stood there and said: "Well, aren't you going to cook them?"

You made what you called an eggless cake, because you only had one egg on the book, so no way could you use eggs for cooking. You did it in the normal way, a little bit of fat rubbed in, for which you used liquid paraffin. This was equal to fat, but was tasteless more or less, and then if you were fortunate, you'd have a bit of fruit. You couldn't complain, because you had no alternative. You either ate it or went hungry. Corned beef you used to mash up with mashed potato, and then you'd make a pie crust and that would make a pie.

I well remember VE night. Churchill came on and announced that the war was over, and the biggest thing that night I think was that no longer did we have to pull blackouts. We put all the lights in the houses on, and nobody would knock on the door and tell you you were showing a chink of light. That night all London was lit up. The celebration was absolutely terrific; all the windows and doors were thrown open. It was a very warm night in May. All the Christmas bunting was festooned outside the houses, and we got hold of a microphone, and trestle tables came from a church hall. Somehow or other we got a party together for the children. Bonfires were lit in the street and it went on for days. The relief was so great.

Speaking for myself, I think the war was a lesson. It gave me a new sense of values, things I'd taken so for granted, even the children you take for granted. You thought of all the trauma you'd been through with them, and it made a closer relationship. I was fortunate enough to have a very good marriage, so the biggest thing in my life was for him to be demobbed, and for us to start to be as a family.

Apply NOW for your new Food Ration Book

DO IT NOW

TAKE a look at your ration book application card (you'll find it at the back of your present ration book). It doesn't look very complicated, does it? You wouldn't think it was very difficult to fill it in correctly? Yet 8,500,000 people filled it in wrong last time! 8,500,000 applications had to be re-done!

That mustn't happen again. It's the duty of every one of us to fill in our postcards carefully to prevent this regrettable waste of time and money.

Follow these instructions as you write and you shouldn't have any difficulty — but do it NOW.

(1) Fill in the REFERENCE LEAF (the postcard in your present ration book) in block letters. Make certain that the postcard is your own.

(2) If the holder of the ration book is under 18 give the date of birth.

(3) *The address at the top should be the same as the address on the front cover.*

(4) *The address at the bottom should be where you are living now or are moving to before the end of July.* Put the name of the Food Office for *this* address on the other side of the postcard.

(5) Fix together the cards for your family with an elastic band or piece of string and *post* them. No stamp is necessary.

(6) If you are not now living at the address shown on the front of your ration book or have changed your name on marriage or are in any doubt at all about how to fill up your card, call at your local Food Office BEFORE filling it in.

(7) If you are the head of a boarding-school or institution with a number of residents using ration books, consult your local Food Office.

 CHECK IT UP! SEE IF IT'S RIGHT! AND POST IT!

THE MINISTRY OF FOOD, LONDON, S.W.1.

Eggless, Fatless Walnut Cake

4 cups flour
1 cup chopped walnuts
1 good cup milk
1 cup sugar
4 teaspoons baking powder
1 good pinch salt

Mix flour, sugar and chopped walnuts together. Add salt and baking powder, then the milk. It should be slightly wetter than an ordinary cake mixture. Leave to rise for 10 minutes. Bake in a greased cake tin in a slow oven till risen and brown.

Mrs. Chaplain

During the first part of the war, I took the air force boys in from Kidbrooke here. I had three boys, and they'd come and they'd go and all the rest. They'd stay about two or three months and then they'd be transferred further on.

I had to give them their breakfast, dinner and tea all for 25/- a week. And I had to do the sheets, but they used to supply the blankets. I had nothing to do with their clothes, that was dealt with by the air force. At the finish I gave it up, because it wasn't worth it.

Emmy Hewlette

When the war broke out, we lived in a block of flats, my husband, two children and my mother-in-law.

We had a shelter with the other people in the flats. Every man, woman, and child was accounted for in the shelter. If people didn't come down to the shelter, the A.R.P. would come up and fetch them.

When the sirens went the boys used to run down sometimes in the nude, in their fright. My mother-in-law didn't trust anyone, so she put all her insurance books, all the jewellery, all what she had, in a bag and we had to carry this bag down each time all the way from the top to the shelter. She wouldn't go without it. Mind you, we didn't like leaving anything, because people would ransack your house. They'd steal anything.

You got frustrated during the war. Actually, I wonder that people who went through the war are as fit in their minds as they are because it could have turned your mind. You didn't have a minute's peace, whether it was night or day.

We never undressed completely for weeks on end. We'd wash one bit, and put those clothes on and the siren would go. Next time, you'd wash another bit. You had to keep clean, but you wouldn't dare have all your clothes off.

The atmosphere in our shelter was good. We used to have a mouth organ playing, and tea and all sorts of things. My mother-in-law didn't care for it much. Our toilet in the shelter was a bucket affair, behind a curtain. We took blankets and pillows and there were old fashioned beds to lie on — bunk beds.

One morning we came out of the shelter and all the roofs of the flats were gone and we'd been bombed out. The A.R.P. came round to see who was missing. They came round with their list to see that everyone got out. My husband was a gas man, so he had to go into bombed out houses and turn the gas off.

We went off to the church hall, but friends took the children. Later we were offered an empty flat. It could hold ten and a half people, so we took our bits and pieces and went up there. The room wasn't too bad. We huddled about in there.

There were bombs and sirens going all the time, so the welfare people said: "The best thing you can do is go to the country." So I had to leave my husband in London, because of his work, and my mother-in-law, because she wouldn't go, she didn't understand.

I was being evacuated to my family home in fact, but we still claimed the money afterwards. My two children went to a neighbour and I went to my own home in a village near Newbury.

Later we got compensation for the flat, because the walls were down and the furniture broken. It took about two years for the men to come and gradually do the building. They built the wall back up in the middle of the room and gave us utility furniture. It was thin like match board. We bought that with the money they gave us. Those men that made it made a fortune during the war, because it was very thin wood.

When we were evacuated, my children and I, we stayed away for about eighteen months. I couldn't work in the village, because there was no work, so I brought my children up to nature study. Of course, when they were older at school, the teachers never knew how the London boys knew so much about the country!

When the bombing got worse, my mother-in-law came to the country as well. A lot of town people didn't like the country. I was alright having a home to go to, but others were put on trains and sent all over the place, up north everywhere. A lot of people came back, although it was a mistake with the children.

When you got evacuated, you'd go to a hall and get provisions. I was alright, but others needed clothes. Where I lived there was a lot of gentry people in the big houses, Wills the tobacco people, the whisky people etc., and they sent clothes for people. The people in the village didn't get them, only the evacuees.

I can tell you a very sad tale about a girl. She was put to Bradford, or somewhere, and we don't really know what happened, but when she came back, she was immoral. It was dreadful. What happened up there, we'll never know. These were the things that were so sad. Why people couldn't have taken in an evacuee girl and looked after her properly, instead of abusing her, I don't know. There were many tales of children being abused, but this one I knew.

During the war everybody had to put an effort into everything, so you didn't have time to be moody, or you didn't have time to think about anything, only about beating it.

Women drove trams and cleaned windows. Today you wouldn't take no notice. I think that must have broken the barrier somehow.

You'd do everything you could for the best, no talking, no saying anything, in case the person sitting next to you was listening.

No one had time. Everyone was busy. It would take all day queueing up to get a bit of dinner, or vegetables, or anything. We had rations, so we knew everyone would get their bit. In the queue we'd talk about things that didn't matter about the war, knitting, or recipes. It was impressed upon you to keep quiet. "Go about your business quietly."

We helped each other then, but after the war it seemed to disappear. I live in a block of flats and it's the loneliest place on God's earth if I can't get out. Some say it's just a living death, because there's no community anymore.

Eliza Eldridge

I couldn't go out to a job myself, because the boy was only three years old and my husband was away. The hospital got in touch with me one day and asked if I could do anything for them.

They wanted me to put up two nurses. "Oh yes," I said, "I could do that." Little did I know what I was in for.

There I was cocking an eye out on them to see if they were happy and also trying to watch the boy.

I had two nurses, Irish they were, lovely girls. I had to make sure their bedroom was clean and I used to cook them a hot meal, when they were on days to come home to of a night time. They did their own washing, I didn't have to do that.

When they were on days, they used to come and have a jaw to me. Brian, my little boy, thought they were wonderful. We used to have tea and biscuits and a jaw.

I can't remember what I got paid, but it was such a struggle, I had to keep on counting it over and over again. We did not go short of anything, because the shop I was with used to say: "Go on, we'll find a couple of bananas for Brian."

I remember one afternoon, I pushed him to Hillingdon, because I thought I might see something going. Well I saw these lovely kippers. The man let me have two pair and me like a silly fool put them on Brian's lap in the push chair, so that I could have a nose round. Suddenly someone said: "Has anybody in this shop got a boy outside?" I said: "Yeah, I have, what's the matter?" "He's alright, but go and see the kippers!" He'd pulled them to pieces!

I looked after the nurses for about two years. Mary's boyfriend got killed and I didn't know what to do to pacify her. She'd sit down and have a cry. A month after it happened, she decided to get transferred back home. The other nurse went as well. They did say to me that they'd been ever so happy with me, I was happy to have them too.

YOU'LL NEVER BE ABLE TO MEND THAT!

MAKE DO AND MEND AND YOU'LL "DO" HIM TOO!

The Squander Bug hates needles and cotton! He wants you to buy new clothes instead of making your old ones last even longer, and saving coupons. Don't listen to him . . . your needle is a weapon of war to-day . . . see that it works full time! With the money saved buy Savings Stamps or Certificates.

Savings Certificates costing 15/- are worth 20/6 in 10 years—increase free of income tax. They can be bought outright, or by instalments with 6d., 2/6 or 5/- Savings Stamps through your Savings Group or Centre or at any Post Office or Trustee Savings Bank. Buy now!

ISSUED BY THE NATIONAL SAVINGS COMMITTEE

Beat the squanderbug with your store cupboard

'All Clear' Sandwiches

Spread fish or meat paste on to bread and margarine. Wash young dandelion leaves and spread on top to make sandwiches.

One Pound of Butter into Two

Warm 1lb of butter to a consistency that will permit of its being beaten up with a fork to a cream, care being taken that it does not oil. On no account must the butter be whisked with an egg whisk. Boil ½ pint milk, with a pinch of salt, and allow it to cool to blood heat. Then stir the milk gradually into the creamed butter. Put in a cool place to set and you will find that you now have 2lb of butter.

"BEING A 'BILLET-MOTHER' KEEPS ME EXTRA BUSY" Hardly time for a bath, yet how one needs it!

MORE people to look after. More beds to make. More rations to get. Very little time to spare for baths! That's why every bath must do a thorough job. Today we live, and often sleep, in crowds. And crowding, hurrying, extra work, all mean more perspiration than usual. So use Lifebuoy Toilet Soap! Even in a quick bath its penetrating lather gets right down into the skin pores and washes out the perspiration deposits that cause " B.O." How fit and fresh you feel after that! And remember, though it deals thoroughly with " B.O." Lifebuoy Toilet Soap is wonderfully kind to the skin.

LESS TIME FOR BATHS
more need for

4D per tablet
(includes purchase tax)

LIFEBUOY TOILET SOAP

LBT 524-836-55   A LEVER PRODUCT

Helen.

When the bombing started, I had to let my two sons go. One was six years old and one was twelve years old. I went up to a friend of mine. She had two sons too, and we let the four of them keep together if they could, knowing each other.

I remember this friend and I went outside and we looked up and saw their smiling faces, in an open-topped bus, with their tickets on with all the evacuees. Inside ourselves we were very upset. I had new suits on the two boys and I made them look smart.

After they left, I could see them in my mind. I kept thinking about them, then I had this letter from a lady, she was a sergeant major's wife. Her and her husband were retired and lived in a big house near Bideford, North Devon, and my children were billetted there. I had a parcel from this lady. Both my son's shirts were returned to me. They'd had a fight and torn all their clothes and she said she wouldn't mend them. So with the bombs dropping and everything, I had to mend them and send them back.

Later on I was evacuated to Devon too, because I wanted to be with my children. There wasn't room for them to be billitted with me, so I was stationed at a cottage with a farm labourer's wife, her husband and two children. My room had been one big room originally, but it had been split in two. It had a plaster board division, that you could hear everything through, and they used to row every night.

I thought I can't stick this anymore, so I went along to the rectory and asked if anything could be done for me. He said: "We'll see what we can do." He got me a place at the rectory.

I was in a room with a thatched roof. There were bare boards and at night I could hear the rats going round. The vicar used to go hunting and he'd bring back a rabbit, skin it and put it at the bottom of the stairs for me to cook. You know what I used to cook it in? A biscuit tin! I don't know why I did all this, but really it was for the children's sake.

I looked after evacuees, when I was evacuated myself. I opened a Saturday morning class for all the evacuees to come in, and I used to sing to them. I loved singing. I was brought up singing, so I was happy doing that.

The kids' foster mothers wanted relief from them, so I took them on Saturday mornings. I got on well with them and I took them out for walks.

There was a river running through the village, and I'm no swimmer, see, so I got the children together and said: "Now listen to me. I can't swim, so if you fall in that river, you drown." They were as good as gold!

You know when I was a child, I never knew what the country was. The first taste I had of the country was being evacuated to North Devon.

I can recollect during the war, being invited out to entertain the soldiers at a party. We had to entertain them by talking to them, before they went out to the front. We, what can I say, lightened their lives and made them happy before they went out.

After the war ended, we were all overjoyed. I went to a friend who lived opposite me and there were people dancing and singing in the street. It was over-enjoyment, but it was wonderful really.

When I first came back, they could only offer me two rooms to take my boys, so a friend of mine got me a flat; she spoke for me. So I had a flat and I had the boys back and that was the happiest time of my life. My husband came back and I got a job with my father as a bookeeper.

I couldn't live through it again, yet I did have some fun with it.

Thank you, Foster-Parents . . . we want more like you!

Some kindly folk have been looking after children from the cities for over six months. Extra work? Yes, they've been a handful! . . . but the foster-parents know they have done the right thing.

And think of all the people who have cause to be thanking the foster-parents. First, the children themselves. They're out of a danger-zone — where desperate peril may come at any minute. And they're healthier and happier. Perhaps they don't say it but they certainly mean "Thank you".

Then their parents. Think what it means to them!

The Government are grateful to all the 20,000 people in Scotland who are so greatly helping the country by looking after evacuated children. But many new volunteers are needed—to share in the present task and to be ready for any crisis that may come. Won't you be one of them? All you need do is enrol your name with the local Authority. You will be doing a real service for the nation. You may be saving a child's life.

The Secretary of State, who has been entrusted by the Government with the conduct of evacuation, asks you urgently to join the Roll of those who are willing to receive children. Please apply to your local Council.

Valerie

I was twelve two days after war was declared. I was living in Ebbw Vale, and we thought it might have been a target, being a big industrial site, but one valley looked pretty much like another, and the bombers found it difficult because of a covering of smog. We were a safe area, and we had evacuees sent to us, so we felt, therefore, we must be safe. I remember seeing a dog-fight in the air over Cardiff, while I was sitting in the bus station, and also a stick of bombs dropped quite near our house at one time, by mistake. That was some planes that had been bombing Liverpool. They came back over the middle of Wales and dropped the bombs up by the reservoirs near us. They went off, crash bang, and frightened us all to death, but apart from that we were alright. Also, we saw the blitz on Swansea, and the blitz on Cardiff, like a giant firework display, with noise like thunder. During that time we spent our nights in the air raid shelter. We didn't have our own, but next door had one and we used to share with them.

We had three evacuees, not all at the same time. The WVS came round and asked if we were able to take anybody. If the mother wasn't out to work, which my mother wasn't, it was more or less obligatory. We volunteered, and they were just brought, by the WVS. I was only thirteen or fourteen then, and my grandmother was living with us, so my mother had my father, me, evacuees and an elderly person to look after. Looking back on it, she did a Trojan's job. She tried to treat them as she would her own children, and it was jolly hard work, because when they first came we would all be doing different shifts. One school started at one o'clock and finished at six, and the other school started at eight and finished at one. Well, poor old mum was everlastingly making meals, and food was in very short supply so it took great ingenuity to find enough to go round. Two of our evacuees came with the most frightful colds. I can remember making them hot milk and honey and putting them to bed with aspirins. They both said that for the first time they felt they were in a family. They were like brothers to me. We grew up together, and that was good. We've kept in touch ever since.

There was an awful feeling at one time, when you really thought the Germans were going to come and invade. In 1941 it was a beautiful summer, but it was eerie. My father was a major in the Home Guard, and one very misty foggy morning, about the end of May, they had a message to say that somebody had landed. In fact some poor old stray German had gone off track and had had to bail out over Chepstow, and they thought this was the beginning of the air-born invasion. My father was on duty that night, and he came tearing up to our house, panting, "I'm going to ring the church bells; I'm going to ring the church bells." We all got out of bed, my mother, myself and our evacuee, all absolutely petrified, shaking with fright and cold. When the church bells rang, the men all emerged out of their little houses, formed the platoon, and they marched up the road in an orderly manner, with pitch forks, shovels, brooms, anything that came to hand. They didn't have any weapons at all, because it was not long after the Home Guard had been formed. My father, who was the leader, had one gun, but I have no idea if it was loaded! We were all watching. It was just us women left together, and I felt a very strong protective feeling towards my mother. I felt that I was young and able-bodied, and I had this feeling that I had to look after her. Probably she was thinking likewise that she had to look after me. Fortunately the whole thing didn't last very long. They all came home from the false alarm footsore and weary and very hungry, about an hour and a half later.

Vera.

We didn't talk about periods. If you had a period you said: "I've got the curse, I'd better go and get myself some S.T.'s or bunnies."

If you were in pain you'd just say: "Oh dear", rubbing your tummy. "Oh like that are you?" "Yes." That would be it.

Gladys.

I can remember wearing washable sanitary towels. They were sheeting twelve inches square about four thicknesses thick and you machined round them. You put tapes on at two diagonal corners. You folded the others into the middle and used them and you had a piece of tape threaded through the loops. When they were dirty, they were put in a bucket with disinfectant and boiled. That was before the first sanitary towels came out. My mother was horrified when the doctor advised me to wear internal ones. She'd been brought up the old way and thought Tampax being inserted meant that the maidenhead was broken! She wanted to know if I was still a virgin?

In a man's job, there's no time for "*not so good days*"

*W*AR work won't wait . . . . . a man's job doesn't allow for feminine disabilities. Tampax—sanitary protection worn internally—has come to the rescue of thousands of women on service. It gives new freedom; complete comfort; assured effectiveness in action. And it's compact and convenient, both for use and disposal.

TAMPAX *Worn Internally*

REG. TRADE MARK

FREE For any further information regarding Tampax please write to THE NURSE, Tampax Ltd., Belvue Road, Northolt, Middlesex. A generous sample will be sent in plain wrapper if you send a postcard with your name and address. This offer does not apply in Eire.

PRICES 7d., 1/2 & 1/9
NEW FAMILY PACK 40 for 6 -
Sold by BOOTS, TIMOTHY WHITES & TAYLORS and other chemists; department stores; WOOLWORTH'S and MARKS & SPENCER LTD SUPPLIED TO THE N.A.A.F.I.

PROPAX Tablets kill the pain and relieve the cause

Engineering.

Lisa Haddon

I had my little boy just as the war started, and then I looked after my nephew as well. When they were five, ready for school, I went out to work with my sister-in-law, doing piece work. I wasn't directed, I volunteered, because I wanted a job. My mother looked after my little boy, and she'd take him to school and pick him up. You had two jobs, on the lathe or the drill. I was doing wheels for trolley tracks, turning them on a lathe, in a big workshop. My husband was working at the gas works, before he went in the army, and he was earning about 30/- a week, while I was earning about £4.00.

A lathe is a machine with a wheel at each end. There's a blade on it, and you put the wheel in the middle, so the blade cuts the metal to the size you want. Then you get your guage and make sure you've got the right size. I made wheels of all sizes. We worked on a long bench, with each person having a lathe. There were about thirty of us. It wasn't very safe, because there was a belt above you which worked the machine and that should have had a guard on it, but it never did. We didn't have any safety until they fought and put a union in.

When you were working on the drill you had a vice at the bottom, then your wheel, and a big wheel at the end. The drill bit was a great a big thing, which would be in the middle. You'd pull that down to the wheel, which was fixed in the vice, drill through it, undo the vice, take your wheel out and put the next one in. Sparks used to fly when you did the drilling, but we never had anything over our hair or eyes. We wore a hat, but it didn't really cover your head. I had a bit of hair in the front of my face, and that caught in the machine. I was sent to hospital, but I wasn't hurt, just frightened. My hair jammed the belt up and the machine stopped.

If you finished the job you were on then you put that down on your sheet, and then you were on ordinary time, until you went on to do something else. You got paid even when you'd finished your job, because it wasn't our fault that there was no work. My sister-in-law worked with me, and we had a system. We were honest, but my husband always reckoned we were fiddling. We'd put down the hour we spent walking around looking for what the foreman wanted us to do next. We never had forewomen, always foremen. They did all the heavy lifting, but if they weren't around you lifted it yourself.

I worked just on four years at this place. I left when my husband came back. He'd been gone four years. The boy was born after he went away. It was funny when he first came back, especially when he took the boy out, because to the boy a soldier was a soldier. He took him to the chemist's shop one day, and he said, "Wait outside, while I go inside, but don't move."

When he came out the boy had gone. He was following another soldier up the road. All soldiers looked alike to him. It was hard for him to adjust, because until then he'd had all women around him. I don't think he ever did adjust. He doesn't get on with his dad now.

The war was good for being able to get money. You lived and laughed. Women worked hard during the war. If you were lucky and could get out, you'd go to the pictures of a night time. I never went dancing, not with my mother you didn't! I did have a little boy after all. I knew some married women who went out with the Yanks. It was funny, because my husband had a friend who was coming home, and he said "Go and see the missus; she'll look after you." He wasn't staying with me, but he came to see me, and that got talked about up and down the street. I was having a soldier in the place! He was there about 6am, yet they saw him. They couldn't understand that my husband had sent him. My sister-in-law gave up her bloke and sent him one of those "Dear John" letters. The bloke was my husband's friend. I didn't know anything about the letter, but my husband did, and he didn't think much of it. All soldiers got one of those letters eventually.

When my husband came home we'd have parties and everything, but when he got into bed of a night time, you'd find him waking up screaming, and you'd have to calm him down. This is what the family don't know. I expect there's a lot of wives like me. You had it on your own, and you'd tell it to the family, and they'd think you were kidding. We had a shelter in our road, and you'd come out of it not knowing if your house had been bombed, but everybody spoke and helped. Now you could be dead in your flat and nobody would know. Why should you have a war to get people to be friendly?

You got friendship out of working. We'd got our independence during the war, and what we didn't have then, we made sure we got after.

Mrs. Jones

I worked at Woolwich dockyard during the First World War. I started work, when I left school at fourteen. That was 1917, the year before the war ended. We were in what they called the propaganda part. We were doing leaflets. They were all printed in German and we had to pack them in bulk and then we had a yellow cord, and we had to put them through this yellow cord and they were taken by our airmen and dropped over Germany.

In 1918, when the war ended, we all went down to the waters edge and we went mad. After the war ended, they kept us on for a little while and they brought us the compasses that the men used to use. We used to scrape the mud off them and some were all bloodstained and we had to get them all cleaned to go back to the stores.

I was living in Clapham with my husband and two children, when the Second World War started. My son was evacuated to Chichester and I went with my daughter down to Bognor. Where we were in Bognor, we were right near the aerodrome, and we hadn't been there long before they started bombing it. So I packed up and came back home again. I also brought my son back to London, because he was being neglected. He'd got sores on his arms and he was lousy, so I had him back home with me in Clapham.

In 1941 my husband got his call up papers to go overseas. He was a sergant major and he was posted out to Africa for the rest of the war training African troops, so I was left in the Clapham flat with the children.

My husband left to go out to the Middle East, and on the way out there the boilers of the ship gave out, so the convoy that was guarding them had to go on and leave them floating about for two days until they could creep back to Scotland, where they'd started from. That put them in an embarrassing position, because no one knew what to do with them, so they were given two days leave.

Well, I'd already said good-bye to my husband and had my final farewell letters from him, and I was in bed with my two children beside me. It was about 2am and it was really quiet. I could hear this pair of army boots coming down the road and opening my gate and I thought: "Who's that?" Well, there was this knock at the door, so I shouted down: "Who's there?" My husband's voice shouted back: "Me." And I said: "Who's me?" I wasn't going to let him in!

When I was living in Clapham, we were having very bad bombings there, so I decided to give up the flat and take the children to live with my mother in New Eltham.

I got work soldering wires for batteries for the aeroplanes at the I.T.T. factory at Footscracy near Sidcup. It was a light very airy room where we worked, not like a factory at all. It was very clean work and I didn't need special clothing or anything.

We worked at a long table and someone brought us the batteries and collected them when they were perfectly finished. We had to solder on very fine wires, finer than a needle, with fine pliers using a magnifying glass. If we didn't solder the wires on properly the foreman would come along and pull them off. Even though they were so fine, he could see them.

I'd start work around 8 in the morning. My mother was looking after my daughter, but she was getting on a bit herself, a bit cantankerous, you know and didn't want to look after her any more. One morning there was a raid and I think perhaps my daughter got a bit hysterical or something, I don't know. But anyway, mum wouldn't look after her anymore and I had to pack up work.

Later on my sister said: "Well, why not work with me in the telephone exchange?" But again my mother said: "I'm not looking after that lot while you go out enjoying yourself." There weren't any nurseries, or at least I didn't have time to enquire if there were, because you were always running!

I did get plenty of money during the war anyway, because my husband's pay came directly to me and the firm he worked for also paid me so much each month.

STANDARD
TELEPHONES &
CABLES, LTD.,

Need intelligent Women with good eye-sight and an interest in electrical apparatus for high grade inspection; day work, 7.15 a.m. to 6.15 p.m., and part-time 7.15 a.m. to 1 p.m. 'or 1.45 p.m. to 6.15 p.m. Also full-time vacancies on assembly. —Please apply in person any day between 9.30 and 11 a.m., and 2 and 4 p.m.

Bessie Miller

When the bombs dropped on London we used to go down into the cellar part of the house. I was expecting my son at the time and my niece from Bristol was staying with me. I used to lie on this camp bed and when the bombs dropped, the top and bottom bits of the bed went up and down with a crash. Once, my niece was looking out the window and saw a bomb drop by Essex Road Station. My neighbour's parents came right down from the bedroom through the floors and were killed. The milkman was missing, later found in a hospital, and three girls at a bus stop — well, they were never found at all. Bombed out of existence. That's when I went to Wales.

We went as we were. We put our coats on and put things in cases. I sent my son out to find a taxi and we headed off to Paddington Station. There was another raid there and we were so glad to get to my sister-in-law in Wales. It was so peaceful and lovely.

My son stayed with one of my sisters, and my two girls lived with people opposite me. I stayed with my sister-in-law. While I lived in Wales, I was conscripted to do war wark, because I was free to do so. One of my sisters and I worked in a factory wiring up gun arms, cockpit lamps and cameras for aeroplanes.

We used to catch the works bus at 6 in the evening

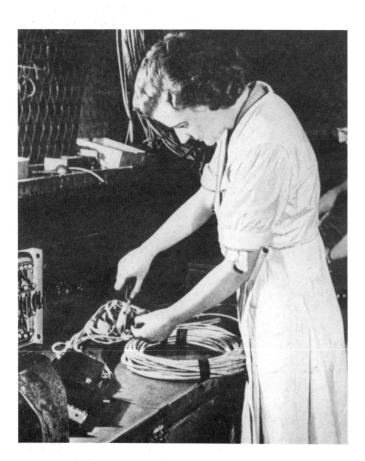

and get home the following morning at 6am. Once the bus broke down at Pontypool and we had to walk all the way from there home in all the ice and snow.

There were about thirty or forty women on my particular bench doing wiring. We had yellow tubing and some of the wires went through that, so that they didn't touch one another. I used to mark the yellow tubing in the book, so we knew how much we had.

Later we were given belts with eyelets. They were for the airmen and we had to splice the ropes, slot them through, and one side had to be $9\frac{1}{4}$ inches and the other $7\frac{3}{4}$ inches. Splicing is threading the ropes through the eyelets and then joining them together. The rope would have three pieces at the end of it and the other rope would too, and you'd fix them over each other. Then you'd pin them together and roll them and you couldn't see where they joined. We also worked on the parts for aeroplanes and one of them was the De Havilland. I was well paid. I enjoyed working and I enjoyed the work.

We used to have a jolly good time laughing and joking. We had a canteen and some people used to get up on the stage in the canteen and sing. We had some lovely singers, and we used to sing all the latest songs. We used to talk about those who had lost families. It was very upsetting at times. Someone would come in and say so and so has lost their father or whatever. It came over the wireless that the Hood had been sunk and some had relations on it.

I had a sister and brother, who worked on T.N.T. It made your hair go funny colours and their skin as well. You couldn't wash it off your hair properly; it tended to stay. You could wash it off your skin, but my brother worked deeply in it and he always looked a funny colour.

Where my sister worked on munitions these German planes came over one day and all the girls started waving to them thinking they were ours, because they'd never had them over before. Then they started dropping bombs and the girls had to fly for cover.

We lived through the war and hoped every day that it would end. At the time I never thought that my wires for the guns would kill people, but I would now. At that time you had to do it, but it's wicked to have to kill anybody. War is a terrible thing, and to think that you are responsible for the death of somebody must be terrible. Those that plan wars ought to be the ones in the firing line. They should fight it out themselves.

The German women were in the same position as us. They had to do what they were told. I used to feel sorry for them, as I did ours.

I remember going from Newport to Bristol once and on the station were all these German boys, who were prisoners, they couldn't have been more than thirteen or fourteen. My heart ached for them and their parents. I hoped and prayed that my children would never kill anybody.

Helen.

I was working at Peek Freans soldering the biscuit tins, before the Second World War. I worked in what was called "the fancy tin shop." It was a huge factory, because they made a lot of biscuits, and they exported a lot as well.

No married women were allowed to work there, so I had to leave. Most firms then, didn't allow you to work, if you were married.

When the war broke out, the firm wrote to me and asked me if I wanted to go back. I had two children, but they were at school and I had a woman who could look after them, so I said "yes".

I started doing my normal job, Peek Freans were still making biscuits you see, but they were soldiers biscuits as well as the others. I also then did other jobs as well, like soldering linings for gas masks, I don't know what you call them, they have a special name, but they were panels for aeroplanes. They'd have the instruments and I'd have to solder them on. All those bits of wire, and I could take as long as I liked, as long as it was done properly. It was people's lives after all.

I used to work from 7.30 in the morning till about 6pm. at night, and if they wanted you to work overtime, you worked till 8 o'clock. If you went in on Saturday you got time and half. I shouldn't think we were getting paid as much as the men. It wasn't much money we got I remember. It wasn't a union firm, so you couldn't go on strike.

They were a fussy firm you know. In the new building they listened to "Music While You Work", but in the old building we had nothing. In fact you weren't even allowed to sing.

We had to wear an overall and they supplied that, and we had to tie our hair back. We were supposed to have a pint of milk a day, but we never got it.

If you swore, I know it sounds funny, but you'd be sent to the manager and you'd be suspended.

Our tea breaks, we got fifteen minutes and we'd talk about where people were last night; if they were courting, who they went out with. There were lots of Americans. I was married, but if you were single, you were all right. You could go out and enjoy yourself in a pub and all that. When my husband came home we'd have a bit of a party make the most of it, if you know what I mean. You felt better if there was company.

The birth rate went up during the war, but it was only natural wasn't it? When the men came home on leave! I knew a few women who had illigitimate kids and people thought they were no good, and as for living with anyone, that was not thought of. People did carry on though, I can't deny it.

I had to leave Peeks after two years, because the bombing got so bad and I went with my kids to Nottingham. Rationing was terrible, but we managed somehow. I used to make my kids bananas out of parsnips. I used to boil them and put the banana essence in them. My kids used to think they had bananas. We did a lot of things like that.

After the war some women stayed on at Peeks, but the men did get their jobs back. During the war we were needed; afterwards it was different. A lot of women did want to leave though, to be with their husbands.

Dorothy Duncan

I was called up from doing ladies handbags. I can remember when we had to register at the Labour Exchange, saying to my father: "I don't want to do war work, Dad, I'd sooner go in the air force, or something like that." And he said: "You're not going in those services; you've got to be at home to look after your mother." She used to have these terrible varicose ulcers and I was the baby you see.

When I registered, they said: "What do you want to be in?" As I couldn't go in the services, I said: "Well, I don't know what I'm going to do. I don't want to go a long way from home, because I have a mother who needs attention." So they said that I could go to the polytechnic and learn how to strip engines. Since I did handbags, I would know how to use my fingers. It was a funny thing, because three girls from my handbag firm were already there when I went. They were surprised to see me.

I got the bus fare from the station to the Southampton Row Polytechnic and the training went on for three months. We had exams. Mind you we didn't see actual objects, all through college. We had lectures, and you had to take notes, but of course, as soon as you started on the job, I used to say to myself: "Oh yes, I 've got that in my notes." I took my notes with me and if I wasn't quite sure, I went down into my locker, got my book out and brought it upstairs, looking at it.

When I first started my job, I was stripping out engines, a filthy mess. We used to take them to pieces all the way to the shell. We had cars, sometimes just the ordinary ten horse power, then the bigger engines twenty-two horse power. These cars were for the army, air force, and also for the naval officers.

After stripping the engine, we'd put the different parts into a de-greaser, and you had to know which parts were yours in this great big de-greaser. It was caustic soda and it boiled. You can imagine, if you got splashed you went straight to the cold tap to wash it off. When the parts were ready, we'd take them out and de-carbon them and then we were ready to rebuild up.

We used to fit the main bearings first, and then go to what we called the big ends on the carmellites. The fly wheel went on next and then the new ring on the fly wheel and all that was screwed onto the crank shaft.

We had to be careful putting in the tappets, because the inspector used to check up on the gaps on our tappets. The cylinder heads and gaskets were the last things to go on.

Sometimes I could do the rebuilding up in under a day, sometimes it was a day and a half. It just depended. We got quite quick at it.

We used to have a target to get so many engines out a week, and you got a bonus. A lot of the girls just would not work for it. What was the good of working, when it would go on income tax? That was the attitude.

We used to start at eight in the morning, and if you were clocked in and ready to start at eight you got a

Learning Details of Engine Construction

56

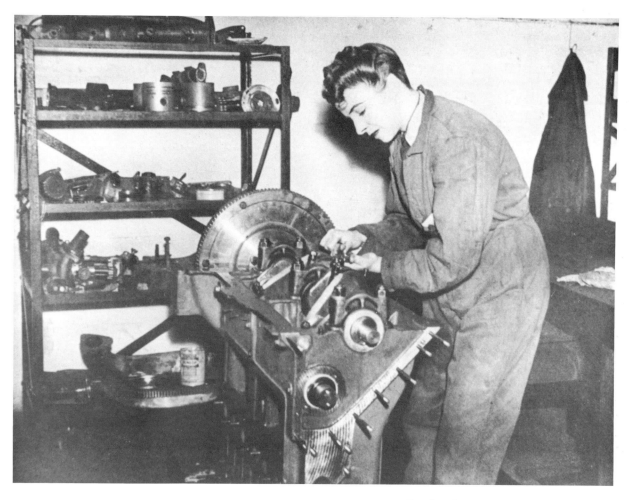

Engine Crank Assembly

bonus of 8/6. If you were five minutes late, you didn't get that, so that was an incentive to try to get you in there.

When I first started the wages were £4 a week, but it gradually went up. The men were paid more than us, although we were doing the same work, but we had to do the work, so you just got on with it.

We used to finish at 8pm. at night sometimes, so we worked a twelve hour day and I had to get home and it took an hour each way. Sometimes I'd have to walk halfway.

We had dungarees, but we had to use our clothing coupons to get them, and we had to have three pairs each. I told the works manager: "It's not very fair us having to use our clothing coupons for our dungarees." Eventually they got organised and issued us with ten extra coupons for overalls and that sort of thing, but when we went to get new overalls, we discovered they'd put up the amount of coupons for them! That was the way it went you see.

We had to take our own soap in from home and we were all rationed on it, so I said to the works manager: "What about us girls having some soap issued to us. We keep bringing it from home, and we're getting no soap to use at home. Just look at our hands now, before we start." He got us some cream to rub into our hands before we started and some soap ration. But, of course, as the fresh ration came up, a lot of the girls would just dip straight in with a great big tin of cream, and then those that needed it from that particular tin had none to use.

Engine Unit stripping down completely an 85 horse power 5 cylinder engine for reconditioning.

To try to keep our clothes free from oil, we took our blouses and skirts off, and kept our undies on, although oil used to still get through. My mum used to say to me: "The state your undies are in!" And I used to say to her: "All I can smell is rotten stinking oil." It used to get right down to my nails and you'd be out in your Sunday best and have to keep your gloves on!

We also had the smell when we were stripping engines and another smell we had was when the boys were revving up engines, and then we got the smell of the exhaust.

We used to get an hour for our lunch and although we had a canteen us girls used to run across to a little restaurant next to Goodge Street station. We used to keep our dungarees on, and the woman reserved a special table for us, because the table cloth got a bit mucky with our dungarees. As soon as we had our lunch that table cloth came off and another one went on.

After we'd had lunch we used to walk to Selfridges and we'd walk right to the stocking counter and the woman knew what we were in for and used to say: "What size." If anyone in civilian clothes went in there, they didn't get any. She'd say: "No, they're for the girls." We did get the best of service and a lot quicker, because we didn't have much time.

We had a shelter at work, and we could use it if we wished, but very few of us did so, because if you'd kept on running down into the shelter, very little work would have got done.

Up Tottenham Court Road there was a big cafe which got a direct hit, and where my engine stand used to be was right by the window. The window was open, because it was summer time. That bomb went off about ten minutes before dinner hour, and everybody just ran. I couldn't feel my legs, and George the foreman called out to me: "What's the matter Doll?" I said: "I can't feel my legs." He said: "Alright, you will in a minute."

After we'd been there about three years, we did manage to get clogs. A chap came around and showed us the clogs and we all went for our sizes. We paid for the clogs, but didn't have to give any coupons up. They were leather uppers, with a bar across the top and wooden soles. It was difficult to walk in them at first, but we gradually got used to it.

I worked there for five years, and all of us girls, when we had children we had trouble. We had difficult times, because those muscles got solid. They wouldn't work. It was because of using the spanner on the blocks for doing up the cylinder heads. Everything had to be secure and on the great big blocks there were four cylinders, the pistons were big, the fly wheel was terrific, and we used to put a nut and bolt in and sling it over the crane and lock it all on to that, and pull it up.

When I finished the work, I didn't miss it. What I missed was the girls. We were all starting to get married and some went to Canada.

Assembling Clutch Unit

CHIESMANS

JUST THE THING FOR THE WAR WORKER

WOMEN'S DUNGAREES made from heavy quality drill in Navy or Khaki with zipp fastening at side and two pockets, as sketch, suitable for munition workers, land army, gardening.

Limited quantity only, unrepeatable.

PRICE **12'6**

Mrs. Grossman

I was asked if I wanted to go into any of the services and I said "No!". I wanted to stay local, so I was sent off to a training centre for six weeks. They taught us how to handle tools, make tin kettles, pans and how to solder. At the end of my training, I had to go for another interview and they said I was to go to Southampton. "No I'm not, because I don't want to leave home." I knew people had got into local places, so I said I'd go there. They said there was no room in those places and I'd have to go to Southampton. "I'm not going to Southampton," I said. I was just a bit awkward I suppose, and eventually they found me a place just outside Oxford. I lived in Oxford, and it was an aerodrome owned by De Havillands and we were repairing Spitfires.

The training school never taught me anything to do with planes, we were just taught to handle tools, and everything was so different at the aerodrome. A man nicknamed "Dingle" (I don't know why he was called that) trained me. He never seemed to be there! I don't know why, but you could never find him. He treated me alright, but he used to think I couldn't do it. He didn't think any of the girls could, but we outshone some of the men!

We worked in hangars with big shutter doors, where they pushed the planes in. I did all sorts of things to repair the Spitfires.

We wore boiler suits, which we had to buy ourselves. They were big massive things with zips at the side and zips up the sleeves. Some girls just wore ordinary trousers, it was a novelty in those days to wear anything like that. We used to tie our hair back to keep it out of the oil and wore our scarves turban style. Once they gave us clogs to wear, but they were so uncomfortable being made of wood and they wouldn't bend. We had to climb up and down ladders and they were dangerous, so we just put them aside and wore our own flat shoes.

We had our own wooden tool box and we had to buy the tools You could pay £8 for a good hammer! We had to buy hammers, drills, spanners, etc. I used to put my name on tools, but they still used to disappear.

People would borrow them and not bring them back. There was a tool shop in the aerodrome, but you had to get things out on a ticket and you'd waste valuable time going to get them and very often they'd say: "Sorry, but we haven't got that."

We had a works coach to take us to work and back, and we had a pass to get into the aerodrome and we clocked in as well. We had to start at 7.30 or 8 in the morning, and some nights it was 9pm. before we got home. At the weekends we'd have Sunday off one week, and Saturday the next. We got good money, overtime, double time on Sundays, and time and half on Saturdays. We always got less than the men, although we were doing the same work. We just accepted it then. I joined the union and paid my 6d a week, but I never went to any union meetings. We had our shop steward — a woman — and we could go to her if we had a grievance.

We had a chargehand in charge of us, and he'd tell us what the work was for the day. We had the work on a sheet and at the end of the day the inspector would come round to check it.

Riveting a Rear Fuselage

Sometimes the planes were very damaged and dirty and we'd have to wash them down first and strip the plane. We had to do that outside and in the winter it was freezing, and we'd have to put our coats on..

We usually worked with a mate and you were given a time to do each job, say two hours, and if you finished early, you got a bonus; if not, you lost it. The girls got more time than the men, which wasn't fair, because we were all quicker than the men! The men used to like having a girl as a mate, because then they got more time.

About twelve people worked on one plane, mostly with your mate, although you could work on the wings or flaps of the plane by yourself, if it was a particular kind of job.

If you were climbing down the fuselage, it would get narrower and narrower, and you got to the point where you could hardly move. You might be on your back bent double, or standing on your head sometimes! We usually climbed inside, because we were more nimble than the men.

I used to climb into the fuselage and patch up and rivet. When you rivet, you had a rivet gun, and the person going into the fuselage would have a metal block inside to flatten it out to fill the hole and hold the patch in. The person with the gun stayed on the outside of the plane. Sometimes the skin of the plane where it had been knocked about, would stretch, so we'd have to put a stiffener in and rivet that. I did similar work on the wings and tail.

I went up twice with the test pilot, when he was testing the planes. The first time I got nervous, because he said to me: "I'm going to turn the engine off!"

Sometimes if they were short of people in the paint shop, I'd go and stick on the red, white and blue slogans and spray them. I'd get covered in paint right down and over everything.

We didn't have many air raids there. If we did, we just pulled the shutters down and carried on working. We used to listen to "Workers Playtime" in the canteen and "Music While You Work". We used to have performers, who performed for us in the canteen. They were rubbish many of them, but you didn't care when you were eating. I used to work with Bob Arnold, who was in "The Archers" and he used to get us to sing along with him in the aerodrome.

I stayed on there for two years after the war. Not many men came to work there, because they were closing it down. At the end of my job in the aerodrome, I took my tools home and you know, they got rusty lying in the shed!

Margaret Kippin

I didn't actually go into war work until 1941, because I was in a reserved occupation. I was fighting like mad with my parents to be allowed to go into the armed forces, because my brothers were all in it. The argument was, well, you're the girl, you should stay at home with mother. Eventually I did win a little bit, because I went into engineering.

I went to a training centre in Surrey. I did six weeks there, but my first week I remember vividly, because we were given a piece of metal and we had to file it into two inch squares. I nearly went bananas, you know. We just stuck it in a vice and filed away. After that we were given a chance of deciding what we'd like to do, and we were given a small mathetmatical test. I was able to go into what they called the inspection side, where you learned to read a micrometer and vernier. They measured things to a thousandth of an inch. After my training, I was sent to a small components factory at Walton-on-Thames. We made parts for the Vickers-Armstrongs, for aircraft.

It was a garage that the owner had converted into engineering. He was one of those people, who made a bomb out of the war actually. He still had his garage on the side.

The conditions were pretty appalling, because it was a corrugated roof, and the rain used to drip down. We did shift work, 6 am till 2pm one week, then 2pm till 10pm the next and 10pm till 6pm the following week. To begin with there were three viewers and I was one of them, one for each shift. He expanded later and then there were more. We weren't allowed to mix with the others in case we passed their work. It was so ridiculous. I remember the boss saying to my husband once, when he came to collect me: "You're a sergeant in the army, you shouldn't let her mix with people." I mean, I had a brother who was flying aircraft, and I knew what the consequences would be if I let the stuff go through that wasn't right.

The foreman would set up the machine for the viewers and bring the first one off to us in the viewing room and we'd measure it. We'd look at the drawing and it would say plus 2 or minus. 3. That meant it could be 2,000th of an inch out, or 3,000ths of an inch either way. I'm talking about 1,000ths of an inch, you know, which is actually sometimes less than a thread of your hair.

When the job was finished, we measured every one up and then you had a little stack with your number on it. I was AWT3 and you stacked them to prove you'd passed them.

The boss opened up the front of his shop for salvage parts and that was really awful, because he had these women and they used to clean parts with that stuff which smelt like nail varnish remover. That added to his coffers.

While I was there my shifts were changed, so I could see all the people who worked there. I knew everyone by name. It was a small place and we had a sweet girl called Molly, who made tea for us, just tea. We had to take everything we wanted to eat. There was one toilet for the whole of the factory, men and women.

The women in the machine shop wrote me a poem for my birthday, and I would often be in the machine shop, when I was on nights, and they would chat to me.

TO MARGARET VIEWER No.3

May this day be most happy for Margaret.
Who's birthday it is as you see.
But to prove why it is so important.
It's because she is just twenty three.

Now this Girl we refer to as Margaret
Is a viewer of greatest renown.
It is to her we go, when we want to know
Is the job right we're doing what ho!

In her room looking calm and collected
She will soon put us right that we know
With her mike in her hand she will say –
    its just grand – or –
My! My! its a thousand below.

Now our Margaret is soon to be married.
It is August as far as we know (!)
Tis lucky the man, she has given her hand,
So Good fortune where'ere they may go.

If there was something you couldn't pass, you sent it back and the machine had to be reset. No one got into trouble. My foreman was a very nice chap, and he tried to get a union going, but of course the boss wouldn't wear it, so he got rid of him. I remember I started a collection for him, and one night I went to work and there was a notice up on the board saying that my collection was illegal. I was so mad, I clocked on, clocked off and walked out. I was a bit bolshy in those days.

After that foreman was given the sack a new chappy came in, and I think I've had about four people in my life who I couldn't get on with, and he was one of them. I think he resented women being able to say that's not right. His attitude was: "You're a woman, you don't know." After all I had the drawing, so I did know.

I'm sure the men got a higher rate than us, but I don't think anybody minded, quite frankly. In those days we accepted it.

Our Shift.
Only two of us actually lived at home, the rest had been drafted and were in digs.
Tragedy had already hit two of the number. The husband of one had been blown to pieces outside a Tube Station on the way home on leave, another girl had lost her fiancée when his ship was sunk. 1942.

Viewers All...
Andy, our charge hand, with Jean, Nesta and myself in early 1942, just outside the factory.

Eventually I wanted to leave. The conditions were appalling. To do this you had to go to a tribunal. I used the health grounds a bit, because it was damp and I had suffered from rheumatism in my youth. My boss being a councillor was on the tribunal, and because I was so bolshy, I think he was glad to get rid of me. If I thought something was unjust, I'd go in with both feet, a bit heavily at times!

Before I went to the tribunal, I was offered a job at Parnell Aircraft, which was a huge purpose built factory on the Kingston bypass. I was offered a job in the drawing room, but I was married, and in the drawing office you couldn't have time off when your husband came home on leave, so I had to go into the machine shop.

That was really boring, because you had boxes and boxes of nuts and you set your micrometer onto the circle thing and you just put the nuts through.

There was everything at this factory: "Workers Playtime", artists coming around and all that sort of stuff, although I never went to any of the concerts.

One interesting thing happened there. We had "Music While You Work" to listen to, and you needed that to keep you going, especially on the night shift. Well, one night the works manager, who lived in a house adjoining the factory, came in and complained. He had guests and the music was keeping them awake!

One thing I did not like, no-one did, was the blackout. Don't forget, trains were blacked out, streets blacked out, stations blacked out, and one morning I had to get a very early train to work. A drunken Canadian soldier got into my carriage and I won't go into the horrible lurid details, but it ended up with me having to get into the next carriage. It was very unpleasant. I had another experience with a Canadian; I'm afraid my experiences with Canadian soldiers weren't very happy.

Mind you our boys could be just as bad. You used to get the old tale: "Well you know, I might be dead tomorrow".

Of course, there were illigimate children during the war, but it was kept quiet. One girl I knew grew up believing her grandmother was her mother and her mother was her aunty.

I always regretted that I didn't go into the forces — WRENS. My brother was training WRENS at the time and I came from a naval family. I was the only girl, with all my brothers and I felt left out.

O.K. I was doing my little bit, as it were, but it wasn't what I really wanted to do. I was angry about that. Nowadays if parents said to a daughter: "You can't do that," she'd go ahead and do it anyway. In those days although you rowed about it, you did in the end succumb to what they wanted you to do.

All together a family reunion in September 1942
The last occasion this was to be so... we had previously
only all been together for a very short period early in
1940.

Within nine months my R.A.F. brother, extreme left,
was killed on a bombing mission.

My Marine brother left England soon afterwards and
we did not see him for nearly three years. The Lorry, in
second photograph, belonged to the Home Guard.

Taken at Chalcot House Surbiton... now pulled down
and is a council housing estate...

Munitions.

Ellen Harbard

I was only 13 at the start of the First World War. We lived in Greenwich then. The headmistress of the school I went to told me I was 14, so I left to do a sewing job. I thought my mum had made a mistake, but when I told her, she said, "No, you're only 13, but go if you want to." I said, "Well, I shall earn some money, shan't I." Anyway the lady next door knew I was only 13, and she gave me away. I had to go back to school for another year, till I was 14.

When I was 15 I had a friend, Ivy. We both lived in Roan Street at the time, and we were going to work at a dressmaking place, only making half a crown a week, learning. It wasn't much money, from 9 in the morning till 6 at night. One day, before we went in there, she said, "Here, I've heard that there's some women down at Abbey Wood, on munitions." I said, "My mother would never let me go there." "You got any money?" she said. I had 6d, and that was the fare, there and back, to the place we worked. So she said, "You've got 6d, I've got a shilling, and it's only 2d to Abbey Wood on the bus. Shall we go? I've heard it's good money." So I said yes. I was very easily led. We went down there, and we saw the man on the gate. He said, "Yes, we do want some girls. How old are you?" We said that we were 15. He sent us along to another office, and they asked if we could start straight away. I said to Ivy, "Whatever will my mother think? I won't get home till 7 o'clock tonight. She'll go mad." Well, when I told my parents, father said, "I'll kill you. Now go inside, before I do." I said, "Oh dad, let me go. Look what I'm going to earn; nearly £4 a week." It was a lot of money in those days. Mum said, "Let her go, let her go, if she thinks it's going to be alright." She was thinking of the money.

"Alright," he said, "but if anything happens to her, I'm going lay it at your shoulders."

After a good few weeks we became lady loaders. They called us lady loaders because we had uniforms. They were a deep yellow, and they did right up to the chin, with a pale blue collar and long sleeves. The shoes were fawn leather.

We had to leave all our things down in the cloakroom, with a woman called Queenie, our supervisor. Everything was left with her, our coats and hats and shoes, and hat pins or hair pins. We had our hair tied back with a big bow.

I was working filling the bullets. You sat there with boxes of empty bullets, and you filled them with powder from a big thing like a dispenser. Then we put them into trays, and a couple of men came and took them away. There were people there working with lyddite and cordite. Their faces all went yellow from the yellow stuff. You wouldn't sit near them, because if your clothes touched them, all the yellow stuff would come out. They had to have a place apart from us.

One day, it was on the 16th of April, some flames started coming along the line towards us, and two men in the shop got hold of us and threw us outside onto the grass. It was raining like the dickens. They knew something was going to happen. The alarm was going, and Queenie, our supervisor, had to go back for her watch. She was blown to pieces. They found her corsets on the line. She was a lovely person, with ginger hair. I'd lost a coat, and I'd lost my tammy hat, and my boots. It was a new coat, a mauve coloured one that my mother had just bought for me. They didn't give us anything, though. We never got a penny. Another friend of mine lived up near Abbey Wood, in the huts, and her mother took us in and gave us tea and something to eat. We were only a bit shaky, but we weren't frightened. We didn't see the worst part of it. We had to go back next day to see what was happening. They laid all the stuff out on the grass, and we were to pick all the good bullets out from the bad bullets. We were only there a fortnight, and then we were put off. I was late home, and my father went to the police station, but nothing was heard. They were waiting for me on the doorstep, and my father said, "Here she is. Take her in and give her a good hiding."

Munitionettes May 1918

Women workers, Woolwich Arsenal, May 1918

Ruth Granville

There weren't the jobs for women before the war like there have been since. No, a woman was expected to stay at home. Employers wouldn't employ married women, because of the break in having children. My husband said to me, "The day you go to work, I'll pack up. If I couldn't afford to keep you, then I shouldn't have married you."

In the First World War I couldn't go out to work, because I had a baby of two and a half. My husband was working in an army factory. He was only getting 26 shillings a week, and he was supposed to send some to me, but I never received it, so I had to do something desperate. I could have got a job in the Arenal, but I would have had to do night work. I wanted my mother to look after my baby so I could go to work, but she refused. She couldn't take on the responsibility of having the baby with the bombing going on. So that stopped that. In the end I bought a Singer Sewing machine, for 2/6- a week, and my sister-in-law got a night dress club going in the Arsenal, where she worked. I'd buy the material, winseyette, feather-stitch them with silk, and on the yoke I'd embroider a flower each side. I did two of those a week, and they were £1 each, material and everything, including what I got for working. I sat until two in the morning, embroidering those nightdresses, so as to get the two done a week. When the war was over, I had such a big circle of customers, that I couldn't cope, so I handed it over to another lady that I knew could do with the work. That's how I kept my money going, because I only had 17/6 a week from the army. I had to pay 7/6 rent a week, and with the other 10/- I had to feed myself and a baby of two and a half.

I wasn't quite fifty when the Second War broke out. The First World War had been shattering, because we'd never known a war before in this country. We were terrified. I remember the Boer War, but then that wasn't in this country. To me South Africa was another world. When this last war came, we weren't prepared for it.

In 1939 I had a big operation, and I was exempted on health grounds from war work. I was going backwards and forwards to Green Lane every night, looking after my mother. She was bed-ridden, so I was looking after her and then coming home through the day to look after my own family. After she died, my husband was working at the glass works in Charlton. He was going into work one night in the blackout, and tripped over the rails where the trucks used to run round. He caught his foot in one rail, fell on the other, and doubled his hand under. He broke every finger in his hand except the thumb. It was two and a half years before he went back to work. During that time my youngest son was at Eltham College. He was doing pretty well, so he said he'd leave school and go to work. I said, "You won't. You'll carry on with your education there. I'll look out for a job."

I went down to Woolwich to the Employment Exchange, and the only thing they could offer me was a job at Graftons engineering works. I'd never been inside an engineering shop, and when I went there, what with the smell of the oil, I nearly fainted, but anyway, I got a job there from 8 in the morning till 8 at night, on the spot welding machine. I used to come backwards and

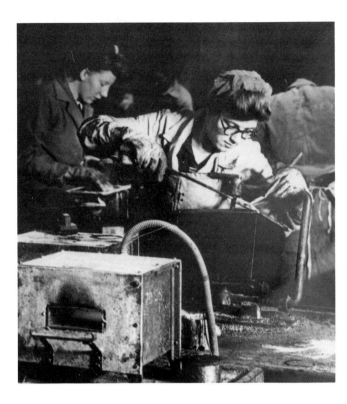

forwards in the blackout, and I couldn't see an inch in front of me to walk home. I got friendly with a younger woman there, and she used to come home with me, to make sure I got there alright. I carried on for about 18 months, and then I decided that when my husband started back to work, I wasn't stopping.

I caused so much trouble there, according to Miss Grafton, that they would have been glad to see the back of me. The girls there were treated disgustingly. They weren't allowed to go to the toilet unless they asked the supervisor, and if you left your overall behind on a Saturday, you had to give a penny to the nurse on Monday to get it back. There were lots of petty things like that. I went to Miss Grafton one day and said I thought the girls ought to have a morning break. The men used to have tea brought into them in the afternoon and morning, and cakes on a trolley, and there was me sitting there watching them, longing for a cup of tea. At my age I could make one at home whenever I wanted one. I got annoyed that the men should be treated differently, so I decided to go to the AEU meeting. So my husband cooked the Sunday dinner, and I went. One of the men had been told to back me up, but he refused to do it, so he got hauled up the next week. Anyway, they accepted me into the union, along with another woman of about 27.

When Miss Grafton called me into her office, I thought, "Well, she's the same age as I am, and I've got nothing to lose, so I'll just tell her what I think."

She said to me, "You know, Mrs Granville, there was never any trouble until you came here." I said to her, "That's where you're wrong. You forget you've got all sorts of people working here now from what you had when you used to start with girls of fourteen, who had to do what they were told. You've got girls of all classes, coming from good jobs in town, being forced to work on munitions." So she said, "Well, what are you doing about it?" I said, "I'm starting a trade union, and I've got enough women to start it."

"What do you want with a trade union?" she said.

"The same as you want with the Masters Federation," I said, "And there's your certificate out there where we clock on. If you're entitled to a trade union, we are."

We were very good; we worked together. At the finish we got a morning break, and a quarter of an hour for coffee or tea. We used to tell them to get back to their machines on time, or else we'd lose the breaks. We had several women in the union. We used to go to the Co-op Hall over in New Eltham for Sunday morning meetings. The men didn't mind, as long as they got a bit more than we did, which they were doing anyway. One day I was put over beside the men on one of the big machines. I guess they thought I was capable of doing anything. They gave me a farthing rise per hour. It was in my pay packet when I got it, and it said, "Please don't mention this to anyone else." I suppose they thought they could do something like that to quieten me down. Nobody was supposed to know what the other person earned. We weren't on piece work, but if you made over a certain number per day of the trigger boxes which I was spot welding for bazooka guns, you got a bonus. The other girls said I was doing too many, and it wasn't good for them.

I was in her office more often than I was at work. After I'd left, my daughter went to work, and the only place she could get was at Grafton's. I said to her, "For goodness sake, don't mention my name." One day, she was sitting in the office with the supervisor, and Miss Grafton walked in. She looked at her, and she said, "How's your mother?" So my daughter said that I was pretty well, looking after her little boy while she got a job. Miss Grafton said, "Tell her that any time she wants a job here, the books are open."

And I felt then that I'd done a good job.

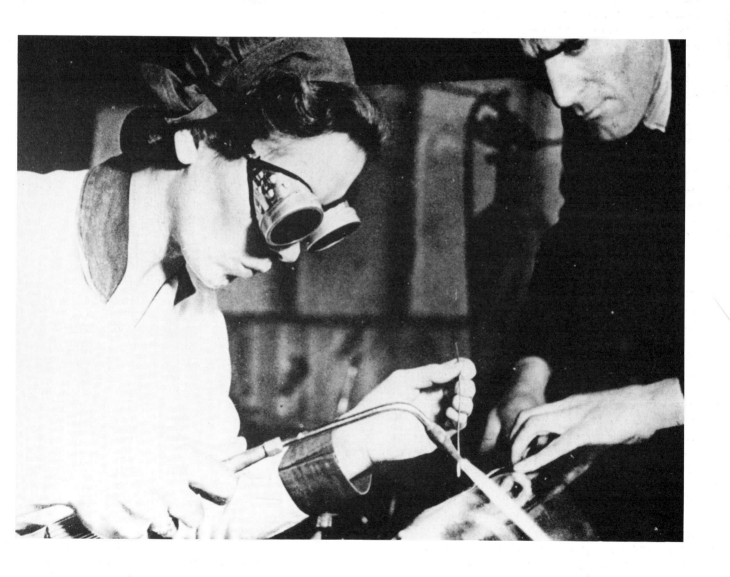

Mrs. Nightingale

I wasn't old enough to work in the First World War. I lived with my grandmother and old aunt then. I can remember the Zeppelin raids. They were like great big silver cigars in the sky, when the search lights were on them. We used to sleep on our desks at school because we were so tired being up half the night watching them. The policemen used to go round on bikes with placards on them saying, "Take Cover," and blowing their whistles. That was nothing like the Second World War.

When the second war broke out I was 35. I was married, and I had two children, a boy of 7 and a girl of 3. My husband was in the Fire Service. He volunteered before war started, so of course, he was called up right away. He had a pretty rough time. When things got bad, my husband was so worried, that we packed up and put our things in store, and I went and lived with my mother on the Downham Estate. My boy was evacuated to Cornwall. It was organised through the school, and some people wouldn't let their children go, but we thought it was safer. I had to pack clothes for him and see him off at the station. When they all went off with their labels on, God it was terrible, really heartbreaking.

It was then that I vent voluntarily to do war work. They were asking for women at the Arsenal, and big hearted me, I thought, "Well, here goes, I'll do my bit for war work." When I went for the medical they said they couldn't have me because I had varicose veins, unless I was prepared to have injections for them. It was a proper medical. I had to take my clothes off, and when they got to my legs, they said, "Ah, veins." I suppose it wouldn't have been good if I'd had to stand for work. They were satisfied when I said I would have the injections.

She's the girl that makes the thing that drills the hole
*   that holds the spring*
That drives the rod that turns the knob that works
the thingumebob.
She's the girl that makes the thing that holds the oil
*   that oils the ring*
That makes the shank that moves the crank that
*   works the thingumebab*
It's a ticklish sort of job,
Making a thingumebob,
Especially when you don't know what it's for!
But it's the girl that makes the thing that drills the
*   hole thta holds the spring*
That works the thingumebob that makes the engines
*   roar.*
And it's the girl that makes the thing that holds the
*   oil that oils the ring*
That works the thingumebob THAT'S GOING TO WIN
*   THE WAR.*

I did a fortnight day and then a fortnight night shift, seven at night till seven in the morning. We used to get on the tram in the morning, and we all used to fall asleep. The conductor would yell out, "Wakey wakey". We clocked in at the Arsenal, and then you had to walk a long way before you got to the particular place where you worked. You went into the dirty side, and had to take off any clothes that were likely to cause sparks, like corsets.

Matches were taken at the gate from anyone who smoked. We had a big kit bag for all our clothes and shoes, and you'd hang them on a rail and they were pulled up on a pulley. Then we stepped over to the clean side. The clean side was in the same room, but it was like up a step. You'd just step over this wooden plank on the floor, when you'd taken your shoes off and put on your plimsolls. We had to wear a mob cap, and big overalls, a fawn colour, like khaki.

We were in a shed and I remember that it was corrugated. It was pretty big. There were about fifty of us mainly women. The overseer was a middle-aged man. We had long benches and when we were on night shift and a raid was on, we'd get the red alert and the light would gradually go down and then it would come up to give us a chance to get off our stools and that, and then it would go out. We used to have to walk miles to the shelters. They were used to have to walk miles to the shelters. They were right away from the danger. They were brick shelters, quite far from the sheds. We had stools at our benches. They were hard. They couldn't make us too comfortable!

The men used to bring the shells for us and put them on the benches. They were big shells, about 12 inches. They'd go in the guns. They'd sit on my bench, and I'd paint these markings on them, and then put them aside. We had to paint most of the shell one colour. It was a yellowy colour, and it dried quickly. Then we'd put the markings on. We never knew what the markings were for. I didn't mind the work. I used to like painting. I used a brush about 2 inches wide. I wasn't on piece work, but I was getting more than my husband. He didn't mind, though.

My mum had an Anderson Shelter, and we always used it. Sometimes you practically lived in it. I always went because of my little girl. We had matresses and deckchairs to make ourselves comfortable, and we'd have flaks and food. The only time I remember an explosion at the Arsenal was one particular weekend when I went down to see my little boy. They had a really bad raid. It was terrific. The bombers had just missed the magazine. When we went in on Monday morning, there were cars standing up on end, and holes everywhere.

We were shut out then, and I didn't go back after that. My husband was so worried about it that he said we had to go down to Cornwall and join the boy.

Marie Maberley

One day I got a letter saying I had been called up to do factory work. I went to the ICI factory in Sutton, making shell cases. They had made packing cases and cardboard before the war, and it was still the same sort of material being used to make the shell cases. We were in one big room. It took about twenty minutes to walk around it. It was so big. We were never told what kind of shells our cases were for: that was secret information. They were the shape of a basin and the size of a soup bowl. The cardboard was pressed into that shape by a machine, and then white tape was glued to the top of each case. The ends of the tape were sewn together to make a loop, and the lady doing the stitching would keep going so you would have a long line of cotton and shell cases together. My job was to cut the cottons, separate them, and pack them in a box to go to the next section. We had to keep an account of how many we did, as we were on piece work. The charge hand would write on a ticket every night how many boxes you did. I had cuts on my thumb, from where I held the scissors, and I had them for years afterwards. Once your fingers got hardened to it you were OK, so you were best to try and struggle on without using plasters, because they got in the way. I used to earn about £12 a week. That was a lot of money then. I was well off. The charge-hand was a woman, and there were some men there who did the jobs that a woman couldn't do, or rather the jobs that a woman wasn't allowed to do then. The windows were very high up and the ventiliation was poor. We had basic toilet facilities, but you were only allowed so long in there. There was a woman who would come and knock on the door if you took too long. If anyone was caught smoking it was instant dismissal, but a lot of them got friendly with her and had the odd cigarette.

Later on I went to work at a factory in South Wimbledon, glueing bits together on model aeroplanes. We had a massive canteen there, and we used to get concerts in it, every two or three months. There'd be comics, and singing, and sketches about Hitler. He was quite a character to imitate, and the ENSA people did it very well. We'd sing war-time patriotic songs; It's a Long Way to Tipperary, We're going to Hang out the Washing on the Seigfried Line, and Lily Marlene.

I volunteered to do fire watching. You wouldn't do all night, just a couple of hours, a few times a week. Each house had a bucket of water and a bucket of sand, provided by the council, outside it. You had to watch for incendiary bombs, and if you saw something coming down, you'd watch where it landed. If it was in someone's back yard, you had to put it out, but you wouldn't run to a bomb; you'd wait until you knew if it would explode. If you couldn't put it out you'd run to the ARP hut to ring the fire brigade. They did a marvellous job really. They didn't get paid, and they were women who didn't need the money.

I remember that everybody helped each other during the war. There was terrific companionship when you borrowed sugar or tea from your neighbour. When I got married, my family and neighbours saved a bit from their rations for me. My aunt made a cake, and she cut out cardboard and painted it blue, and she put silver dots for the sky and little aeroplanes, because my husband was in the airforce. Instead of icing, it had this cardboard cover. I had a long white lace wedding dress, and we had the reception in my mother-in-law's neighbour's house. All the walls were down upstairs. It was just a large room with plain floorboards. People loaned tables and chairs. For a honeymoon we went to stay with a posh aunt in Hayes for a week. My uncle had saved up his petrol ration, and he'd take us out somewhere every evening.

During the war women accepted the work they had to do. When I was making the shell cases, I had that feeling that I was going to kill someone, but I knew that if I didn't do it, someone else would. You didn't let it get to you that it was going to kill women and children. You would go beserk if you did. You felt that it would fall over a military target. We found out later that it was just as bad on their side as ours.

MY SKIN IS HEALED NOW – *says this War Worker*

New Discovery of Science clears
Acne, Spots, Rashes, Etc.

The greatest advance in skin healing in 50 years. This soothing antiseptic balm is white, non-staining, invisible on the skin and pleasant to use. Yet ten times more deadly to germs than Carbolic Ointment. 'Valderma' was tested in hospitals; is now recommended by eminent Skin Specialists. It heals spots, rashes, sores, boils, impetigo, barbers rash, etc. Makes skin clear and healthy often in only a few days.

"I felt I had to write to tell you how much I owe to your Valderma Antiseptic Balm. I am on a job with oil that gets on one's face and I developed acne. Valderma ended it and keeps me free from trouble. Our Nurse at the factory has started to recommend it." Miss M.H.

At Boots, Timothy Whites & Taylors and best chemists or send postal order for full size jar 2/- post free. Dae Health Laboratories Ltd. (Dept.79N), 25/27 Berners St., London, W. 1.

VALDERMA ANTISEPTIC BALM

Craven 'A'

will not affect your throat

10 for 8½d
20 for 1/5
Made specially to prevent sore throats

ON SALE AT ALL BARS IN THIS THEATRE

Carreras Ltd.—150 years' Reputation for Quality

Evelyn Ritchie

I was training to be a nurse, when all of a sudden the war came. I started training when I first left school. They needed nurses, but they wouldn't let me sit the exam. The matron called me into her office and said I had to finish. I told them I didn't mind what I did as long as I did something. I didn't want to be at home all the time, and I didn't want to be beholden to anybody. They had creches in the hospital for the children, so all the time I was training there was a place for my little girl, which I paid for. I said I wouldn't go to another job unless the little girl was settled, so the hospital said that if I did munitions there would be a place for her in a nursery. I used to take her to the nursery at Maida Vale before 8am., because I had to be at work by then, in Park Royal.

There were two of us in the factory, doing the paint spraying of the bombs. There was a special building for the paints, away from the factory. We had a locker room where we got changed: we had to wear clogs and big overalls, and a hat like a chef's hat. We wore masks like doctors' masks. The fumes were bad, but you got used to it. We had a phone, so if we needed anything we could phone down to the factory. We didn't have anybody supervising us. We knew what we had to do, and just did it. We were trusted.

The bombs used to arrive on lorries, and the old men and boys used to lift them off on a crane. We'd tell them where we wanted them. We used to do all different sorts of bombs. Some were about 4 feet long, and some were in pieces. We sprayed them and then they went to another part of the factory to be put together. Someone would put a number on the bomb, so we'd know what colour to paint it. There was red, black, orange or green, and the paint was in big cannisters, with a spray thing coming out of the top. There were two great big ovens in the room, from the ceiling to the floor. We'd spray the bombs and then put them in the oven. A man would come and take them out, and when they came out they were too hot to spray again, so we'd leave them for the next day. We used to have to do our quota of work for the day, and if we got through it we could go home early. The woman who worked with me had her child in the same nursery as mine. Next day we would carry on from where we were the day before, and at some time during the day a new delivery of bombs would come, and they'd take the finished ones away. I was well off during the war and the work was quite interesting, but I wasn't doing it by choice. I would rather have done my examination and been a nurse.

Mrs. Stanley

Before the Second World War I had ten years at Seimans. I loved working at Seimans because they were a nice sporty lot of girls there. During the morning break we used to go upstairs to the toilets and have our lunch, and one of the girls would have been to a show up the Empire, or a picture, and perhaps there might have been some chorus girls in them. We'd hear all about it, and you can imagine us all dancing!

I came out of Seimans when the war was on. I signed on at the Labour Exchange and they gave me a paper to go to the Arsenal straight away. I was poked in there doing a month on night shift and a month on day shift. We got good money at the Arsenal: well, I considered it good. I got ten guineas a week. I worked in the sheds, on a platform raised off the ground. They called that the dirty side. There was a road, with a platform built over it, and we walked on that. You had special shoes and special overalls which wouldn't cause friction. You weren't allowed to keep watches on, or clips in your hair. You could wear your wedding ring, because that wasn't steel. We had a special uniform. We had coats made out of the material men's flannel trousers are made of, and big overalls: they did look pretty, right down to your ankles, and a mob cap and a leather shoe.

I was making bullets and gun powder. We used to make cartridges for guns for the navy. You had a bag, with a big bundle of cordite in it, and then the gun powder went in on top. We used to sew the bags up. They went into the cartridges first, and the shell went in behind.

I was six months pregnant, when I had a doodle bug drop at the side of me. I was going up the garden path, and I got caught outside the air raid shelter and knocked down by a bit of rafter on my head. I don't remember any more about that, until someone found me. I had the baby that same week, and it was still-born. I stopped at home for a little while until I got over that, and then they poked me in the Arsenal again. You couldn't have any fun in the Arsenal, with the air raids coming over all the time. We used to get warnings in there, when the rest of the people didn't. We had a shelter there, and we had to put covers over the ammunition, but I used to take a cover off and use it over me.

WAR WORK'S TRUE STORIES, No 1

Marion finds a fighting job, too—

1. When Marion's boy-friend was called up, *she* wanted to be in it too. So she asked the Employment Exchange about War Work.

2. In next to no time they had fixed her up at a Government Training Centre, learning to make munitions.

3. And before long she was in an important war job. At last she felt she was really 'doing her bit."

4. Jim *was* proud of her when he came home on leave! He knows how much equipment counts in modern warfare!

There's War Work waiting for YOU! Go to your local office of the Ministry of Labour and National Service, they will tell you how best to serve your country.

Your duty now is **WAR WORK**

ISSUED BY THE MINISTRY OF LABOUR AND NATIONAL SERVICE

Mrs Jones.

I was living in London when the Second World War broke out, working in the Express Dairy in New Oxford Street, as a waitress. We had tea shops then. I was there when war broke out. We heard it on the wireless, and everybody went mad. My friend had two little children, and she didn't want to stay in London, because we thought they were going to come next day and bomb us. I left with her. I went in to work on the Monday morning to tell them I was going, and then we travelled home, to South Wales.

I went to work in the ordnance factory in Bridgend. Going to Bridgend was hectic because you had to have an hour and a half's ride on the bus. A special bus took you, the works bus, for three different shifts. When you were on the day shift you had to start at 4 o'clock in the morning, and you had to be early to clock in. You used to knock off at 2 o'clock on that shift. The night shift used to be coming off as we arrived, and they'd go back on our bus. We had overalls to put on, and we had to be searched. You couldn't wear clips in your hair, no metal, so you couldn't wear a watch, and you'd have to take your rings off. We worked with yellow powder, which made everything go yellow. Our overalls were supposed to be white, like drill. You had to cover your hair, otherwise you would be blonde. Even your hair went yellow. The powder used to get into everywhere. It was horrible A lot of people couldn't stand it. They were ill, and they were removed then. You had to do your turn in the powder shop, and we used to try and get out of it. It used to be terrible, especially if it was at night, because everything was closed in at night. We would be in there dealing it out for people to use. We wore masks in there, because you didn't want it to go down your throat.

I can't remember what we were doing with the yellow

powder, but we worked in little cubicles. You'd have to be very quick. That's why they put women on the job. They were more nimble than the men. There were lots of people in charge, walking round seeing that you were doing your work. Some of them were not very nice. They'd be watching you at the breaks.

Eventually they opened a factory at Rhigos, near Hirwaun, my village, and I went to work there. There was no travelling to Bridgend after that. We were putting the tops on bullets. We didn't have any training. You were just shown, and you had to do it. They used to tell you to take time in the beginning, and then you'd speed you. You could speak to the girl next to you and potter on.

Beverley Langford

During the First World War, I was in the gunpowder shed at Abbey Wood, filling the cordite bags that go in the back of the shells. I volunteered to work there to help with the war. I earned good money there, about £3 a week. The bags were made of serge. They were cream and red, and had five holes in them which you filled with gunpowder and then stitched along the top. The powder came in little silver jars, and we had a silver shovel to get it out. The powder would be brought to us so we wouldn't be kept waiting, since we were on piece work. I would write down how many I'd done for the day, so I knew how much money I was to get.

It was such good money that I didn't want to leave, but then the shed next to us got blown up. Some of the girls were blinded, and some were injured, and my dad said he'd rather have no money and have me safe. When the shed got blown up we got no warning. In fact, someone said there was a Belgian spy there, but I never heard the truth of it, because I left.

Woolwich Arsenal –   *Danger Buildings – May 1918*

AGE EXCHANGE REMINISCENCE BOOKS

The Age Exchange is a theatre and publishing company working with London pensioners on shows and books which record their life experience and their current concerns.

It is a feature of all these books that the contributions come from many pensioners, are lively and easy to read, conversational in style, and lavishly illustrated with photographs and line drawings of the time. All the stories are told in the original words, from transcribed tapes, or pensioners' written contributions.

The following books are already available:

"FIFTY YEARS AGO": Memories of the 1930s, a collage of stories and photographs of day-to-day life around 1933. £2.95

"GOOD MORNING CHILDREN": Schooldays in the 1920s and 30s. Fascinating reading and delightful photographs for today's and yesterday's school children. £3.95

"ACROSS THE IRISH SEA": Memories of London Pensioners. This is a moving account of the decision to leave family and home in rural Ireland in 1930s–1950s to seek work in London. Irish people recount their experiences of finding new friends and a place to live, settling down and how they feel about growing old 'over here'. £6.95

"A PLACE TO STAY": memories of pensioners from many lands. Ethnic elders from the Caribbean, the Asian sub-continent, the Far East, Cyprus and Poland tell of their arrival in Britain and their experience of growing old here. The stories are told in English and in the mother tongues. £3.95

"ALL OUR CHRISTMASES": a book of Christmas memories by London pensioners. £2.95

"MY FIRST JOB": Pensioners' memories of starting work in the 1920s and 30s. £2.95

"CAN WE AFFORD THE DOCTOR?" was a frequent cry before the days of the NHS. This book examines health and social welfare in the early part of this century when people often had to rely on their own resources and remedies to cope with illness or disability. Childhood diseases, infectious diseases, accidents and more serious illnesses are recalled. Doctors and nurses remember their early years of service and conditions in homes and hospitals. The book has many photographs and illustrations. £3.95

"MANY HAPPY RETIREMENTS". "For anyone who has sat through conventional pre-retirement courses, being lectured at by experts, relief is at hand. Wisely used, the refreshing new source material in this lovely book from Age Exchange, with its case studies, transcripts and dramatised cameos, is guaranteed to revitalise even the dullest course." Michael Pilch, Vice President, Pre-Retirement Association. £3.95

"THE TIME OF OUR LIVES", is a compilation of memories of leisure time in the 1920s and 30s. Spare time was limited and money always in short supply, but the stories reveal the energy and enterprise of young people who made their own entertainment in the days before television. Pensioners who are now in their seventies recall vividly the comedy of their courting days, the dance, cinema, rambling, cycling and outings of their youth. Generously illustrated with photographs and line drawings, this makes good reading for all ages. £3.95

"ON THE RIVER": The recollections of older Londoners who have lived by and worked on the River Thames. Their stories recapture the sense of bustle and industry when the river was London's main thoroughfare and the docks were a crucial source of livelihood for thousands of families. The book contains over 100 full page photographs of the river in its heyday. £12.95

"GOODNIGHT CHILDREN EVERYWHERE": A remarkable collection of first hand experiences of evacuation in the Second World War. The contributors speak honestly, in many cases for the first time, about the upheaval they went through as children, illustrating their stories with letters they wrote at the time and the photos of themselves which were taken to send home to their parents. Over 250 superb photographs. £15.95 (hardback)

"WHEN WE WERE YOUNG": A delightful anthology of photographs and memories of growing up in the West Country. A record of Age Exchange's South Somerset project in five villages, with reflections on the process from pensioners, staff and children, this book also provides a useful working model for other reminiscence projects. £3.95

"LIVING THROUGH THE BLITZ": Londoners' memories of broken nights in and out of the shelter, being bombed out, hazardous journeys to work, queuing for rationed food, and hunting for shrapnel among the ruins. £4.95

"JUST LIKE THE COUNTRY": The story of families who moved from inner city tenement blocks to the new cottage estates of outer London in the inter-war period. They talk of the challenge involved in making a new life in their "homes fit for heroes", and the sense of nostalgia they felt for the old ways and communities they had left behind. £6.95

"OUR LOVELY HOPS": Memories of hop-picking in Kent, plus over 100 delightful photos of work and play "down hopping." £6.95

THERE ARE SPECIAL PRICES FOR O.A.Ps who wish to order any or all of these books. In all cases postage and packing is extra.

If you would like to order any of the above titles please write to Age Exchange, 11 Blackheath Village, London SE3 9LA. If readers are interested in hiring our touring exhibitions of photographs, they should contact us at the above address, or telephone 081 318 9105.

Produced by Oakdale Printing Co. Ltd. TEL: (0202) 675706 FAX: (0202) 666442